D1199182

Unleashing the Velcro Dog

Training Your Agility Dog to Love Working at a Distance

Jane Simmons-Moake

FlashPaws Productions

Unleashing the Velcro Dog

Training Your Agility Dog to Love Working at a Distance

Book Design/Illustrator: *Jane Simmons-Moake*

Photographs: *Jane Simmons-Moake, unless otherwise noted*

Editors: *Gordon Simmons-Moake, Susan Roehm, Maggie Downey, Lois Williams, Paula Parrish, and Jan Downey*

Cover photo: *MACH5 ADCH FlashPaws Runaround Sue XF, SACH, JCH, RCH, GCH-Bronze, ADHF, 20" National Champion - 2006 AKC Agility Invitational. Photo by Randall Knapp*

Production Assistant: *Jan Downey*

Cover Design: *Raul Carrera*

FlashPaws Productions
7714 Rolling Fork Lane
Houston, TX 77040-3432
www.flashpaws.com
Email: info@flashpaws.com

ISBN 978-0-9674929-3-3
Library of Congress Control Number: 2007905365

*This book is based on **Unleashing the Velcro Dog** columns first published by **Clean Run – The Magazine for Dog Agility Enthusiasts**.*

Printed in the United States of America

Contents

Acknowledgments

Sincere thanks to the following people who helped make this book possible:

- Gordon Simmons-Moake, Susan Roehm, Lois Williams, Maggie Downey, Paula Parrish, and Jan Downey for their expert help in reviewing the manuscript.

- Randall Knapp for his exceptional photographic work and for always being there to help with anything and everything.

- Linda Wakefield for her valuable consultations on book design and production.

- Jan Downey for keeping everything at FlashPaws on track while I worked to finish this project.

- Our wonderful students, instructors, and their dogs who make it all worthwhile by providing continuous support and inspiration.

Dogs Appearing in this Book:

Holly
OTCH, MACH11, ADCH FlashPaws Holly-
wood Hotshot UDX2, SACH, JCH, RCH, JCH,
BDA-CD, ADHF, OD, AKC US World Team
Member 1996 and 1997
owned by Jane Simmons-Moake

Susie
MACH5, ADCH FlashPaws Runaround Sue
XF, SACH, GCH - Bronze, JCH, RCH, ADHF,
20" National Champion - 2006 AKC Agility
Invitational
owned by Jane Simmons-Moake

Joni
MACH Wedgewood FlashPaws Ready to
Rock XF, SACH, RCH, MAD
owned by Jane Simmons-Moake

Blitza
MACH3, ADCH Blitza vom Ronin Haus
SCH, TM-Bronze, OF, CGC
owned by Gordon Simmons-Moake

Kenda
Sandstorm Can't Stop Now MX, MXJ, OF
owned by Jan Downey

Billie
Plails Billie'on Dollar Baby AX, AXJ, OF
owned by Randall Knapp

About This Book

Do you long for a dog that will soar accurately and enthusiastically through the most challenging agility course, regardless of your choice of handling position? If so, you have come to the right place. This book focuses on retraining your joined-at-the-hip Velcro dog to both enjoy and excel at working away from you.

The Joys and Benefits of Distance Handling

At some point in your dog's agility career, it becomes clear that the ability to handle at a distance would be a tremendous asset, if not a necessity. Distance handling is a requirement in some non-regular classes such as Gamblers and FAST. However, it also affords a competitive advantage for excelling on most other types of courses. Distance skills provide tools to smoothly handle courses with handler restrictions, such as when the arrangement of adjacent obstacles prevents your being close to the obstacle of your choice. Distance skills also allow your dog to perform sequences smoothly and at his fastest possible speed, while not being limited by yours.

One of the greatest advantages of having an arsenal of distance skills at your disposal is the enormous flexibility you have when choosing a handling strategy. If you're tied to a particular position on an obstacle or sequence, it severely limits your handling options.

For example, it is an advantage to be able to run ahead (or hang back) on contact obstacles or weave poles when it helps your dog best see the upcoming line of obstacles, or helps to cue a turn. Handling from a wide lateral position can help you take a shorter path than your dog, thus allowing you to take full advantage of his speed. These and many more competitive advantages are available to you with a distance-trained dog.

The training methods used to retrain a dyed-in-the-wool Velcro dog are very similar to those you would use to start a new agility partner on the right track. Nevertheless, it will take longer to retrain your Velcro dog than to teach a new pup astutely from the start. The longer you have been rewarding your partner for trotting obediently beside you, the longer it will take to persuade him to do otherwise. Still, with perseverance and a step-by-step plan, your efforts with ultimately pay off!

Foundation, Foundation, Foundation

The three most important keys to success in real estate are: location, location, location. Likewise, the three most important keys to success in agility—and especially distance handling—are: foundation, foundation, foundation. If you skip or gloss over your foundation training, your dog's performances will suffer. For example, if you have previously only asked your dog to perform contacts, weave poles, the table, or any other obstacle while you remain enslaved to a specific position beside him, then he may no longer know how to perform the obstacle if you vary your handling position. At best, you may get a slow, unsure performance with many approval-seeking head-checks.

The first essential, foundation-training step in your quest for a distance-trained dog is to teach him to perform each individual obstacle at a distance with optimal speed and accuracy. Next, you will progress to short, simple sequences at a distance, while maintaining all of your hard-trained speed and accuracy. Gradually, you will master longer and more complex sequences at a distance from a variety of handling positions.

Chapter One

Tools and Concepts

Before undertaking any of the exercises in this book, you may find it helpful to acquire some helpful training tools and familiarize yourself with some of the concepts that will be referred to in future chapters.

Training Tools

Having the right tools at your disposal can help your dog learn faster and with a greater degree of accuracy. What's more, they can make agility training more rewarding for both you and your dog.

Treats and Toys

Ideally, you will want to use a variety of both treats and toys during your training sessions. A great variety of rewards makes training more fun and unpredictable. Your dog never knows what he will be trading his behavior for; therefore, he is likely to remain eager, alert, and "in the game."

During your training, make it a point to couple the delivery of your rewards with sincere praise. (Dogs are great truth detectives and can tell when you are "phoning it in.") If you let the cookie do the work for you without incorporating praise, affection, and play, you will be no more interesting to your dog than a treat that someone has dropped on the ground.

Choose highly palatable training treats that are small enough for your dog to eat quickly without chewing, such as bits of cheese, chicken, or hot dogs. For some of your obstacle training it helps to use treats that will stick to surfaces. There are many commercial dog treats as well as acceptable human foods that meet this description. Experiment with a variety to see which work best for you and your dog.

Many owners lament that their dogs are not interested in toys. The best time to cultivate an interest in toys is the moment your pup enters your household, although it is never too late to work on it. Training with toys may require more energy on your part, but often pays off with increased drive and a closer bond between dog and trainer. Tugging and retrieving make you—the trainer—a large part of the reward which helps promote solid teamwork.

A Velcro dog will benefit from rewards thrown ahead of him on the course rather than rewards delivered near the handler's body. Toys or balls are ideal for this purpose.

Food Container

A multipurpose motivator that's especially useful for dogs that are not toy- or ball-oriented is a plastic food container, as shown in **Figure 1-1.** Fill the container with treats and throw it as you would a toy or ball to encourage your dog to work ahead of you.

Figure 1-1

When the dog touches the container, you can run up, open the container, and give the dog a treat. Although you could throw food without a container, it is not advisable. The food is usually too small for the dog to see immediately so you would be encouraging your dog to spend time sniffing the ground looking for food.

Be sure to choose an appropriately-sized container for your dog. It should be large enough that it cannot be swallowed. Poking a few holes in the lid will release the scent of the food and make the container a more interesting chase object. If you fill the container with hard treats, you can shake it to make an attention-getting sound. If you prefer to reward with soft food, you can fill the container with a mixture of both soft and hard treats.

Targets

One of the most useful tools for encouraging your dog to work at a distance is a target. A good target for food-motivated dogs is a plastic margarine container lid **(Figure 1-2)** with a small piece of food in the center. Placing the food on a visible target of this kind rather than directly on the ground prevents the

Figure 1-2

dog from learning to sniff and root around for hidden food. When using a target, it is important to never allow your dog to cheat by rewarding himself without having performed the desired behavior. To prevent possible cheating, you must have a very reliable recall. Alternatively, you could have a friend ready to cover the food and prevent the dog from rewarding himself should he attempt to cheat. Another solution is to use a closed food container instead of an open target.

Wire Guides

For your distance-training work you will need a supply of 3 or 4 wire guides **(Figure 1-3).** These tent-like training aids are indispensable for training weave poles, as well as for training independent approaches to all of the obstacles. You can also use them for blocking approaches to incorrect obstacles. As an added bonus, placing one or more of these guides over a jump bar can encourage your dog to pick up his feet as he jumps.

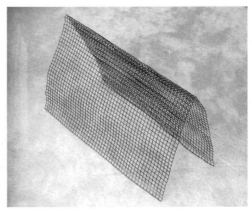

Figure 1-3

You can easily make a supply of guides by cutting and folding wire fencing material to the desired height and length. (Be sure to trim off any sharp edges!) The green-coated, very-small-mesh variety of fencing material called *hardware cloth* holds up particularly well over time and blends into the background of your training area.

For general use, guides that are 12"-15" high and 2'- 3' in length are the most useful. You may also want to have a few giant-sized guides (2' high by 3' long) for large or rambunctious dogs that fail to see the purpose of the smaller guides.

Contact Channel Guides

An especially useful and easy-to-construct training aid is a pair of contact channel guides as shown in **Figure 1-4.** These boards are used to keep your dog's rear from coming off contact ramps sideways. Without the boards to help him be successful, you dog may feel the need to slow down to prevent his rear from falling off to one side. Using the boards helps maintain top speed while teaching your dog to control his rear on the descent. The boards we use in our classes are 36" long by 12" high. An 8" x 8" metal bracket helps keep them upright.

Figure 1-4

Contact Hoops

If you have a tall or long-strided dog, or if you ask your dog to perform running contacts, you may want to have some training hoops available for your contact training **(Figure 1-5).** Training hoops help pattern the dog to lower his head and touch the upside and downside contacts of the dogwalk, seesaw, and A-frame. Depending on your training area, you can use base-mounted or stick-in-the-ground hoops.

Figure 1-5

Clip Stick

A clip stick is a dowel with a clip on one end to which you can attach treats or small toys **(Figure 1-6).** If you have a dog that needs improvement on weave-pole performance, such as drive, head position or efficient footwork, you may want to use a clip stick. The use of the clip stick is described in detail in ***Chapter 6: Weave Poles at a Distance.***

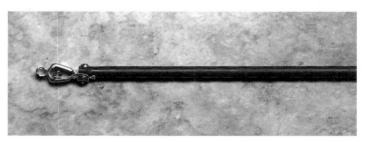

Figure 1-6

Training and Handling Principles

When working at a distance, it will help to keep in mind some important principles:

◆ **Give a command for every obstacle and for every turn you want your dog to make.** As you begin to work farther away from your dog, your verbal commands take on an importance that is equal to or greater than the importance of your body cues. Giving a command for every obstacle and every turn leaves nothing to chance. It also provides you with the best opportunity for smooth, fast performances and tight turns.

◆ **Keep your movements smooth and continuous.** Choppy handling, with rough starts and stops, is likely to direct your dog's attention toward you, which can result in choppy performances from your dog.

◆ Well-timed verbal commands and body cues are crucial when working at a distance. **Work with a friend to keep your timing sharp and pro-active.**

The "Path"

Many trainers fail to recognize the importance of the handler's body language in communicating direction to their dogs. Dogs communicate with each other through body language; therefore, it is only natural that our dogs rely heavily on our body cues for information about where to go.

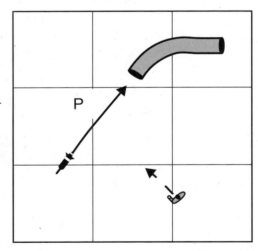

Figure 1-7

Generally speaking, when you want to push your dog laterally outward, or to keep him at a lateral distance from you, your entire body should face perpendicular to the dog's path, that is, midway between your dog's current position and the next obstacle you want him to take, as shown in **Figure 1-7**. This important distance cue is called "pushing to the path." In your training, it may help to place a path marker such as a traffic cone or a stick-in-the-ground driveway marker in a strategic position to help remind you to face the correct direction. In this book, path markers are indicated in the illustrations by the letter P.

When you want to bring your dog in laterally closer or to keep him close laterally once he is there, you should face parallel to the path you want him to take.

When handing at a distance, if you face the next obstacle rather than the path, you are giving an ambiguous cue to your dog. The farther away you are from your dog and the more options that are available to him, the more apparent this will become. The concept of pushing to the path may sound strange at first, but don't dismiss it as voodoo until you've tried it. It really works! (My husband, a research physicist, even claims that it has a solid foundation in physics.) What's more, unlike cues you may have used when running beside your dog, pushing to the path works **wherever** you and your dog are on a course. Do some experiments of your own to see what your dog sees when you face the path versus when you face the obstacle. You will soon become a believer.

Another way to help you think about facing the path is to think of the air between you and your dog as a clear, solid mass—like an ice cube! Alternatively, you could think of it as the air being a protective "force-field" or large "buffer zone." By pressing on the air in a specific direction you can influence your dog's path, keeping him from coming back toward you.

Conventions

Throughout this book, all equipment setups are on a 10' grid; that is, each line on the grid is separated by a distance of 10'.

When not illustrated by dog and handler icons, the letter H signifies the handler and the letter D signifies the dog.

Chapter Two

Tunnels at a Distance

Starting with tunnels is a good idea because they are easy to master at a distance. Moreover, the ability to send and call to tunnels on a course is one of the most useful and commonly applicable distance skills you will use on almost any course.

Your goal is to be able to call and send your dog to the tunnel from a wide variety of angles and distances. Ideally, you will gradually increase the distance until your dog is confident with being called and sent to the tunnel on one command and signal from a distance of 30'. This is your first essential step in teaching your dog that you want him to work at his maximum speed—not try to match yours. The earlier in your training you can convey this, the better.

It's best to start with calling rather than sending since most dogs are naturally faster and more confident running toward you than away from you. It's also easier to be successful with calling than with sending, and it is important to build on success.

Calling to Tunnels

Using the setup shown in **Figure 2-1,** place your dog in a sit-stay about 12' from the tunnel entrance (position D1) and lead out to the opposite side. (If your dog isn't rock-solid on his stay, opt instead for a friend to hold and restrain him while keeping him excited. This will help build speed and impulsion and will help prevent attitude problems stemming from repeatedly fixing broken stays.) Call your dog through the tunnel using one command and signal. As soon as he enters the tunnel, move to the side (so that you will not be in your dog's path as he exits) and turn your back to the tunnel. As he exits, throw a ball, toy, or food container straight ahead and release him with a command to *Get It.*

If successful, incrementally increase the angle at which your dog must approach the tunnel (positions D2 through D9), while you remain in line with the exit. Eventually, vary your position and your dog's position so that you can call him through a tunnel regardless of where you or your dog is situated **(Figure 2-2).** To progress, increase your dog's distance from the tunnel until he is starting 30' away from the tunnel entrance.

Through all of these exercises, you should signal with the hand closest to your dog and face the dog's path rather than the obstacle. When calling to obstacles, the path is midway between your dog's position and the obstacle you want him to take.

If at any time your dog bypasses the tunnel, rather than going through it, look down at your feet to see if you were

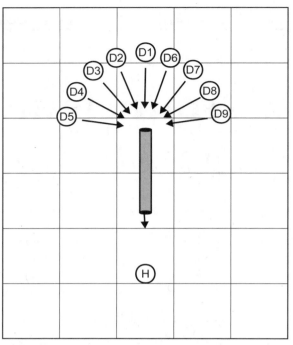

Figure 2-1

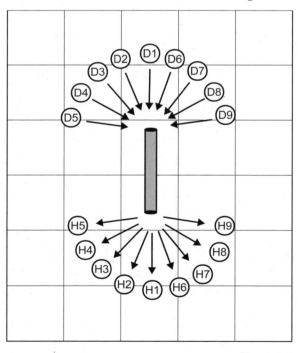

Figure 2-2

facing the path. If your dog bypasses the opening despite good handling on your part, make the exercise easier by starting your dog closer to the tunnel opening and/or by positioning barriers (such as wire guides or baby gates) to either side of the tunnel opening.

Sending to Tunnels

Once you are successful at calling, begin sending. There are two ways to work on sending your dog to obstacles—using an offset start or sending from your side. It's important to master both skills.

Offset Starts to Tunnels

When you send your dog to an obstacle using an offset start, you will leave your dog and lead out to a strategic lateral handling position. (Once again, if your dog is not solid on his stay or lacks motivation, disregard the stay and use a friend to restrain, excite, and launch your dog, if necessary.) Arrange the tunnel as shown in **Figure 2-3**.

Set your dog up for speed and success by using an incentive to encourage him to run ahead of you to the tunnel. This could be a toy or food placed on a target about 3' from the tunnel exit. Alternatively, you could have someone ready to throw a toy or treat container as your dog exits.

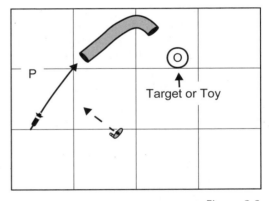

Figure 2-3

For your first attempt, start next to your dog and perform a run-by as you have customarily done in the past. As your dog exits, release him to the target or toy with a release to *Get It*. Now your dog knows what awaits him at the end of the tunnel.

Next, position yourself and your dog for an offset start as shown in Figure 2-3. Face your body and signal (using the hand closest to your dog) toward the path, as shown by path marker P. Give your command for the tunnel and start taking small steps, signaling and walking toward the path (not the tunnel!) until your dog commits to the obstacle. Reward generously for success.

Some dogs may bypass the tunnel and head straight for the target. Prevent your dog from rewarding himself and take steps to prevent him from making a beeline to the target on the next attempt. This may require angling the tunnel exit so the target is not visible to the dog until he exits the tunnel. You could also use a barrier such as a baby gate or wire guides (as illustrated in **Chapter 1: Tools and Concepts).** Alternatively, have a friend enthusiastically launch your dog using a tab until he is committed to the tunnel. However you accomplish it, going through the tunnel will be rewarding for your dog. He will soon realize that his prize is forthcoming only after following your obstacle command.

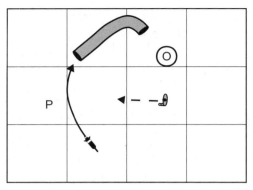

Figure 2-4

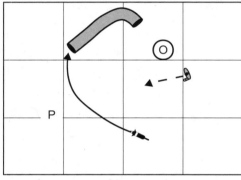

Figure 2-5

On subsequent tries, gradually increase the angle of approach **(Figures 2-4 and 2-5)** as you also increase your dog's starting distance from the tunnel.

Sending to Tunnels From Your Side

Using the progression shown in **Figures 2-6 through 2-8,** send your dog to the tunnel from your side with increasing angles and distances. When sending from your side you should face parallel to the path you want your dog to take, as shown by the dashed handler arrows.

As your dog catches on, you will need to take fewer steps parallel to the path before your dog locks onto the tunnel. Gradually increase your starting distance from the tunnel until you are sending your dog from a distance of 30'.

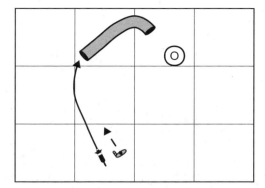

Figure 2-6

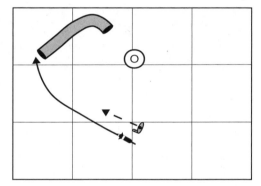

Figure 2-7

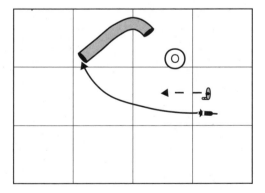

Figure 2-8

RANDALL KNAPP

Chapter Three

Jumps at a Distance

J umps comprise a large percentage of the obstacles on an agility course. In light of the enormous payback you will receive, it is only fitting that you start distance training on jumps early in your obstacle training sessions. The earlier you introduce this concept, the more likely it will be that your dog will drive ahead, power himself (rather than be powered by your running steps), and run at his fastest speed while negotiating jump sequences.

To build foundation skills, your goal is to be able to call and send your dog to any type of jump from a wide variety of angles and distances. You will gradually increase the distance until your dog is confident being called and sent to jumps on one command and signal from a distance of 30'.

To help ensure early success, begin your training with winged jumps rather than wingless jumps. It is less likely your dog will bypass jumps with wings, especially at increasing angles of approach. It is also a good idea to start with the jumps set low, so your dog is less likely to drop a bar. It is also easier for your dog to be fast, confident, and successful. Later, when your dog masters the skill at a low height, you can begin to raise the jumps.

As with all obstacles, it is best to start with calling rather than sending since most dogs are naturally faster and more confident running toward you rather than away from you.

Calling Over Jumps

Using the setup shown in **Figure 3-1**, place your dog in a sit-stay at position D1 and lead out to the opposite side of the jump at position H1. (If your dog isn't solid on his stay or if he lacks motivation, opt instead for a friend to hold and restrain him while fueling his excitement.) Call your dog over the jump using one command and signal. Throw a ball, toy, or food container as he clears the bar with a simultaneous release to *Get It.*

If successful, incrementally increase the angle at which your dog must approach the jump (positions D2 through D7), while you remain in line with your dog and the jump (positions H2 through H7, respectively).

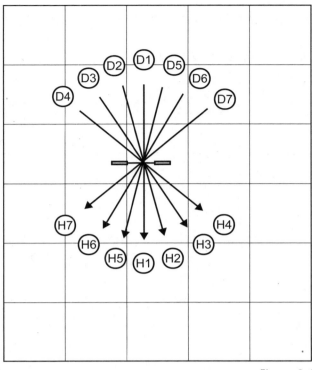

Figure 3-1

Increase your distance as well as your dog's distance until you are each 30' feet from opposite sides of the jump.

IMPORTANT NOTE: *Speed is an essential part of your dog's performance on all exercises. No ho-hum trotting or uninspired performances are allowed! Your goal is to make explosive performances business-as-usual for your dog. You can help encourage maximum speed by conveying an air of confidence, urgency, and enthusiasm in your voice. If your dog is not soaring toward the jump at his fastest speed, do something different on your next attempt to ensure that your dog is faster. For example, excite him with a game of tug or keep-away, then have a friend restrain him as you move to the other side of the jump, teasing him with his toy or treat.*

Sending Over Jumps

Once you are successful at calling, start sending. There are two ways to work on sending your dog to obstacles:

♦ Sending from your side

♦ Using an offset start

Sending to Jumps From Your Side

Begin with the setup shown in **Figure 3-2.** Place a highly coveted treat on a large, visible target—a paper plate works well. If your dog prefers toys, place one on the ground instead of using a target. To build drive, you could opt to throw a toy or food container if you can get it to land directly opposite the dog on the other side of the jump—you don't want to set your dog up to cheat by running around the jump. Show your dog the incentive before starting the exercise. To build drive, you can restrain him by the collar or tab and excite him with a motivating phrase such as "Are you ready?" Add to the excitement by stationing a friend near the target to help point it out. The friend can also help prevent your dog from rewarding himself if he decides to run around the jump instead of jumping over it.

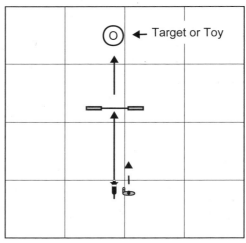

Figure 3-2

When your dog is eager and focused on the reward, give your command and signal for the jump using the hand closest to the dog. The moment he takes off for the jump, release him to the reward with a command to *Get It*.

Using the progression shown in **Figures 3-3 and 3-4**, send your dog to the jump with increasing angles of approach. When sending from your side, face parallel to the path you want your dog to take, as shown by the handler arrows. Follow the same progression in the opposite direction off your right. Gradually increase your starting distance from the jump until you are sending your dog from a distance of 30'.

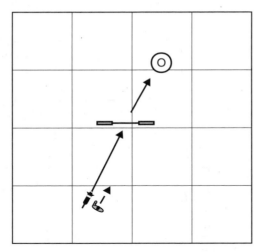
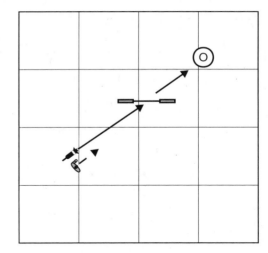

Figure 3-3   *Figure 3-4*

Next, alternate between sending your dog to the target with calling your dog to come to you after the jump. Take steps to prevent your dog from rewarding himself if he ignores your command to come and heads for the target. Provide big rewards for successfully taking the jump and coming directly to you. Eventually, fade away the target so that you are sending your dog to the jump from your side without a visible lure.

Offset Starts to Jumps

When you send your dog to a jump via an offset start (also referred to as a lateral lead-out), you will leave your dog in a sit-stay and place yourself in a strategic lateral handling position. When doing so, the jump will not be positioned directly between you and your dog, Instead, your dog will "take a line" to the jump from your signal and body position. This is an essential skill for distance handling that affords you tremendous flexibility in where you position yourself on a course.

Place a target or toy and your dog as shown in **Figure 3-5**. (Once again, if your dog is not absolutely solid on his stay or lacks motivation, disregard the stay and use a friend to excite, restrain, and launch, if necessary.) Lead out past the jump and to the side as shown (H1) and face path marker P1. In doing so, you are facing the dog's path, or roughly halfway between your dog's current position and the next obstacle you want him to take. Extend your signaling hand (the hand closest to your dog) toward P1 then give your command for the jump. When your dog takes off for the jump, face your body and signal (H2) toward P2 and release to the reward with a command to *Get It*. Path marker P2 is roughly halfway between the dog's current position (midway over the jump) and the place you want him to go (the reward).

On subsequent tries, gradually decrease the amount of your lead-out to increase the distance your dog must work ahead of you **(Figures 3-6 and 3-7)**. Continue to increase your lateral distance from

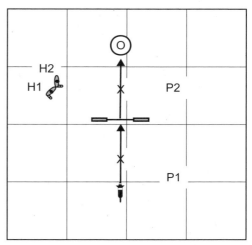

Figure 3-5

your dog until you are successful working 30' to the side of him. Be sure to also work the mirror image of this exercise progression off your left.

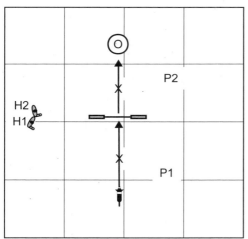

Figure 3-6

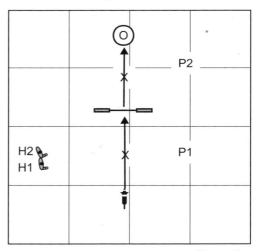

Figure 3-7

Next, alternate between sending your dog to the target with calling your dog to come to you after the jump. As before, take steps to prevent your dog from self-rewarding if he ignores your command to come and heads for the target. Provide big rewards for successfully taking the jump and coming directly to you. Eventually, fade the target so that your dog is performing offset starts without a visible lure and is coming directly to you after the jump for his reward.

How to Progress

Once successful with calling and sending to single winged jumps, repeat all of the exercises with other types of jumps such as wingless jumps, panel jumps, and spreads. Start with the height set low then gradually increase it as your dog gains confidence. Remember to insist on speed and enthusiasm always!

Chapter Four

Contact Obstacles at a Distance

Are you a slave to the contact obstacles? If you are unsure of the answer to this question, try the following experiment: Place a chair in line with the center of the dogwalk, about 20' away from the obstacle. Sit in the chair (or for a lesser challenge, stand in front of it). From this position, send your dog to perform the dogwalk.

- ◆ Did your dog run immediately toward the obstacle and ascend without cutting the up ramp?

- ◆ Did he race across the obstacle at his fastest speed without looking at you for direction?

- ◆ Did he run to his goal position (for example, two-on/two-off) without slowing down?

- ◆ Did he hold his position (if part of the job description) until released with a release word, an obstacle command, or a directional such as *Come* or *Out*?

Chances are you answered "No" to at least one of these questions. If so, it is time to train your dog to ace the contact obstacles regardless of your handling position. This is absolutely essential if you want to achieve maximum flexibility in choosing your handling position on a course.

It's true that you won't be handling your dog from a chair when you compete. Yet you will benefit greatly from the ability to hang back, run ahead, handle wide, or pull away from the obstacle while your dog does his job at top speed and with perfect accuracy.

As with all of your distance work thus far, it will take longer to achieve solid results with a Velcro dog that has been trained to rely on your pace and position on the dogwalk, than with a pup that has never learned that your position and speed have any relevance to his job. Take heart—even if your companion was previously trained to stick by your side, he can eventually be taught the new rules of the game.

To handle contacts at a distance, it is highly recommended that you choose a stop-at-the-bottom performance criterion for your dog rather than a running contact. This will be a much more concrete and under-standable skill for your dog, considering that you will not be nearby to assist his performance with body cues. Once the stop-at-the-bottom behavior has been established, you can always choose to interrupt your downside contact command with the command for the next obstacle to achieve the appearance of a running contact. For most dogs, I rec-ommend the two-feet-on/two-feet-off position for the dogwalk and the A-frame, and either the two-feet-on/two-feet-off or four-feet-on (at the end of the plank) position for the seesaw.

Establishing a Fast, Independent, and Accurate Performance

Before you can train your dog's performance, you need to define what you want. Here is my definition for the dogwalk:

> *When given a command for the dogwalk, the dog will race at full speed to the obstacle, ascend the up ramp squarely, hitting the contact, and race across the ramps. Before he begins his descent, you will give your command for his contact position (such as **Place, Spot, or Bottom**). Your dog will continue to race at full speed to the two-on/two-off position at the bottom of the down ramp. He will remain glued to that position until released with an obstacle com-mand, a directional command (such as **Come, Out, Left, or Right**), or a release word. Most importantly, he will perform the obstacle in this manner regardless of your handling position, body movements, or any other distracting condition.*

A good way to encourage your dog to run quickly to his two-on/two-off position, regardless of whether or not you accompany him, is to use a strong motivator such as a food-loaded target placed on the ground. Position it 8″ or so from the downside contact, depending on the size of your dog. Start with a visible target such as a white plastic food-container lid. Station a friend near the target as illustrated by position A in **Figure 4-1**.

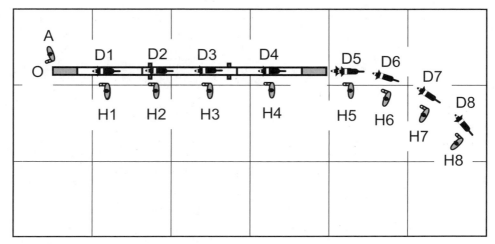

Figure 4-1

It can also be very beneficial to place contact channel boards (also affectionately called "butt boards") against the sides of the dogwalk down ramp. These boards make it possible for your dog to run as fast as possible, without having his rear swing to the side **(Figure 4-2).** For all of the exercises it is also helpful to position wire guides against the sides of the up ramp entrance as shown in **Figure 4-3**. These will ensure your dog performs a straight approach to the obstacle, without cutting the upside.

Pick up your dog and place him at D1 on the down ramp (with you at position H1), a few feet from the target, as shown in Figure 4-1. (If your dog is too big to lift, start on the ground at D5 (with you at position H5— just show him the target before you start.) Excite your dog by restraining him from the target and encouraging him with motivational phrases such as "Are you ready?" or "Where's your Place?" as your friend also encourages him and points out the target. Give your downside command, (for example, *Place*), and encourage him to race at full speed down the ramp. **Don't try to match your dog's pace!** You are in all likelihood retraining your dog to understand that your position and movement has nothing whatsoever to do with his performance on the dogwalk. The last place you want to be during this process is right next to your dog, stopping when and where you want him to stop!

Figure 4-2

Figure 4-3

Have your friend reinforce your dog for waiting in the two-on/two-off position by placing additional "wait" cookies on the target once he has reached a stop. If your dog releases himself without a command, your friend can immediately place your dog back in the correct position. Release with a *Come* command and ensure that he comes quickly on your first and only command.

Next, progressively backchain your starting position as shown in Figure 4-1, varying your handling path and speed on each of your successive attempts. Sometimes hang back, sometimes race ahead as fast as possible, sometimes handle wide, sometimes stop abruptly, and sometimes pull away. Eventually you should even be able to run backwards or pivot and run in the opposite direction from your dog while he speeds toward his two-on/two-off position. To help maximize speed and impulsion, restrain your dog and use verbal encouragement with each attempt.

When your dog is running full-speed to his spot without help from your assistant, you can gradually fade away the assistant's presence. Then, fade the target by using progressively less visible targets. (For example, if you have been using a white plastic target, you can progress to a large clear or translucent plastic target, and then progress to a small clear target.) Next, alternate between targets with and without food, and eventually progress to using no targets at all. Be prepared, however, to bring back the targets (and possibly your friend) if you observe your dog slowing down or acting uncertain about the requirements of his job.

Calling to Contact Obstacles

Once your dog is running quickly to his position and holding it without help from you or your friend, you can begin calling to the obstacle.

Using the setup shown in **Figure 4-4**, place your dog in a sit-stay at position D1 and lead out to the opposite end of the dogwalk at position H. (If your dog isn't rock-solid on his stay or if he lacks motivation, have a friend hold and restrain him while fueling his excitement.) Call your dog to the dogwalk with one enthusiastic command and signal.

If successful, incrementally increase the angle at which your dog must approach the dogwalk (positions D2 through D9), while you remain at position H. When calling your dog to the obstacle, remember to signal with the hand closest to your dog, and face your body toward his path (a point halfway between the dog's current position and the entrance to the dogwalk). Next, vary your position along with your dog's position as shown in **Figure 4-5**. Progress until you can place your dog in any of the positions—D1 through D9—and successfully call your dog over the dogwalk from any of the handler positions—H1 though H9.

Gradually increase your distance and your dog's distance until you are both 30' from the dogwalk.

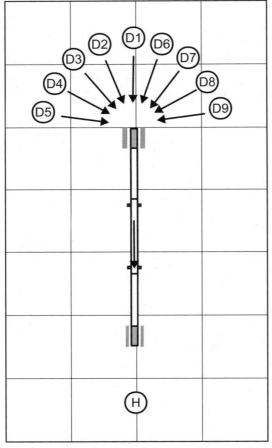

Figure 4-4

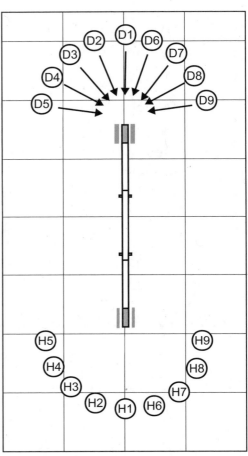

Figure 4-5

Sending to Contact Obstacles

Once you are successful at calling, start sending. Practice sending from an offset start and from your side, as described below.

Offset Starts to Contacts

When you send your dog to a contact obstacle via an offset start, you will leave your dog in a sit-stay and move laterally to place yourself in a strategic handling position.

Start by positioning your dog as shown in **Figure 4-6**. If your dog is not solid on his stay or lacks motivation, disregard the stay and use a friend to excite, restrain, and launch, if necessary. Speed is essential throughout all of these exercises!

Lead out to position H1 as shown and face the dog's path, indicated by the X on the dog's path line. Extend your signaling arm (the

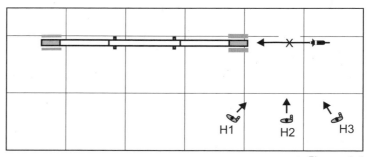

Figure 4-6

arm closest to your dog) and face your body toward the X, then give your command for the dogwalk. If your dog is new to this exercise, it may help to take a few steps toward the X to help him establish the line you want him to take. When he catches on to the game, a single step forward toward the path marker will be all that he needs.

On subsequent repetitions, gradually decrease the amount of your lead-out (positions H2 and H3) to make the offset start more challenging. Gradually increase your lateral distance from your dog until you are successful working 30' from his side. Be sure to also work the mirror image of this exercise progression off your left.

Next, increase your dog's angle of approach to the dogwalk and follow the progressions shown in **Figures 4-7 and 4-8**.

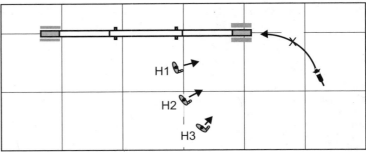

Figure 4-7

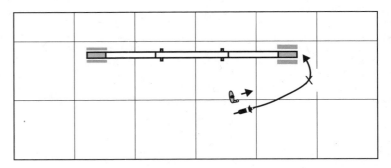

Figure 4-8

Sending to Contacts From Your Side

Begin with the setup shown in **Figure 4-9**. When sending the dog from your side, face parallel to the path you want him to take, as shown by the handler arrows and the X along the dog's path. On subsequent tries, gradually increase the distance between your starting position and the dogwalk up ramp as shown in **Figures 4-10 and 4-11**. Be sure to also work the mirror image of this exercise progression off your left.

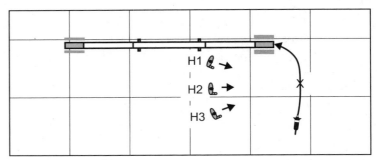

Figure 4-9

Figure 4-10

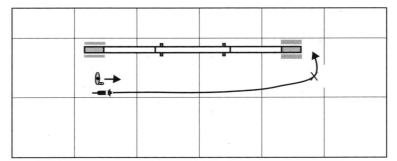

Figure 4-11

Proofing for Reliability

Once you can call and send to the dogwalk with speed and accuracy from a variety of dog and handler positions, it is time to proof him for distracting conditions. In competition, your dog will be running in a very exciting atmosphere. When you are handling at a distance you will not be close by to focus your dog's attention away from distractions. You will need to train him to ignore all distractions and perform the contact obstacles with speed and accuracy regardless of your handling distance.

To simulate the excitement of competition, provide your own distractions as your dog performs the dogwalk. For example, after your dog has come to a stop in the two-feet-off downside position, drop a toy (or food-container for dogs that prefer food) a few feet from the end of the contact. If he waits, praise and then immediately release to the toy with an enthusiastic command to *Get It*. If he breaks, at the precise moment of his infraction give a non-emotional verbal correction such as *Wrong, Oops,* or *Uh-Oh* and prevent him from rewarding himself. The verbal correction will help communicate to the dog exactly what was incorrect about what he just did, thus helping your training progress more quickly. Follow with an immediate chance to get it right under easier conditions (such as using a target and/or dropping the distracting toy or food container farther away from the plank).

Progress to throwing the toy, then throwing the toy excitedly, then throwing the toy excitedly with cheering, after your dog has come to a stop in the two-feet-off position. Praise and release to the toy with a command to *Get It.*

Next, progress to distracting your dog *as he runs down* the descent ramp. First, drop the toy unexcitedly while your dog is running down the ramp. If successful, progress to eventually throwing the toy excitedly with cheering as your dog runs down the ramp. (If you have already weaned off the use of targets, you may need to return to using them temporarily if your dog comes up short of the desired position or loses speed on the down ramp.)

Next, have one or more friends help distract your dog while he is performing the contacts and you are handling at a distance. All is fair except anything that might frighten or injure the dog. Eventually, your dog should perform the contacts with speed, focus, and accuracy while you and your friends are cheering, clapping, throwing balls, toys, and dropping or throwing containers of food.

How to Progress

Follow the same sequence of exercises with the seesaw and A-frame.

If you are asking for a two-on/two-off performance on the seesaw, the procedure is the same as the one you followed for the dogwalk. If asking for a four-on performance, simply replace the use of a target on the ground with a sticky food treat placed at the very end of the seesaw plank. A four-on performance is recommended for dogs under 40-50 pounds. (When a lightweight dog runs as fast as possible to a two-off position, it is likely that his front feet may be suspended in air well before the plank hits the ground. A four-on performance is a safer choice, since it ensures that all feet will be in contact with the board when it hits the ground.)

When training the A-frame at a distance, it may be helpful to use contact channel boards as shown in **Figure 4-12** to keep the dog's rear straight when racing down the descent ramp.

Figure 4-12

If you have chosen a running contact performance on any of the contact obstacles, use a training hoop on the down ramp and place your target or toy several feet from the base of the obstacle.

On all exercises, if you notice any decrease in speed or accuracy, back up a step and make sure you achieve an improved performance on the next try.

Chapter Five

The Pause Table
at a Distance

D oes your dog insist that you escort him to the pause table and remain with him until the end of the count? If so, you may want to consider unlocking the chains that make you a slave to the table!

The advantages of distance training on the pause table are many. Your efforts will lead to your dog running to the table at his fastest speed, without being limited by yours. As your dog quickly assumes the correct table position, you can race ahead to reposition yourself ahead of your dog during the 5-second count. At the judge's command to *Go*, you can immediately call your dog through the next series of obstacles without ambiguity and at your dog's top speed.

As with all of your distance work thus far, it will take longer to achieve solid results with a dog that has been trained to rely on your pace and position near the table, than with a dog that has never learned that your position and speed have any relevance to his job.

An exemplary table performance can be divided into two behaviors:

♦   Running at top speed to the table and jumping on it

♦   Assuming the desired position (sit or down) immediately upon command and maintaining it until released

For purposes of training and shaping behavior, it is very helpful to define your commands to separate these two components. For example, the *Table* command means "run at full speed toward the table, jump on it, and remain there (in any position) until receiving another command or a release word from the handler."

To communicate the desired position, the handler gives the command to *Sit* or *Down* when the dog has left the ground for the table. The dog must assume the position instantly and remain there until released with another command or a release word. By keeping the *Table* command and the *Sit* or *Down* commands separate, it is much easier to communicate and reinforce each desired behavior.

Sit and Down at a Distance

To be able to handle the pause table at a distance, your dog must immediately sit or down on the table on your command—regardless of your handling position. It is assumed your dog already has a fast response to the sit and down commands, provided you are close to your dog. If not, be sure to master these behaviors up close before attempting to gain distance.

It is best to work on a fast sit and down on a variety of ground surfaces (without using a table) away from your agility training. Moreover, it's best to have your dog begin the exercise from a standing position for the fastest and most efficient transfer to his table performances. The dog should move immediately into position from a stand and not assume an intermediary position (such as a sit before moving into a down), which wastes time.

To prevent your dog from coming toward you on his sit or down as you increase your distance from him, try one of the following:

♦ Put up a baby gate between rooms in your house and leave your dog in a standing position on one side of the gate.

♦ Use a three-sided box made from wire guides as shown in **Figure 5-1**.

♦ Have a friend stand behind your dog and restrain him on leash while you add distance. Your friend can also help guide the dog into the correct position if necessary.

Figure 5-1

Keep in mind throughout that speed is essential. Use excitement in your voice and make the exercise seem like a fun game. Eventually you can selectively reward for only excellent or improved speed.

Calling to the Pause Table

To begin calling to the pause table, use the setup shown in **Figure 5-2**. Place a food-loaded target near the back half of the table—far enough back so that your dog will need to jump on the table to get his reward.

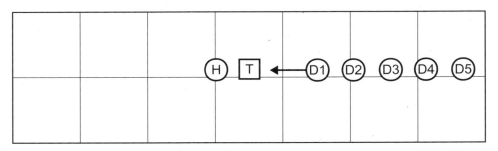

Figure 5-2

Place him in a sit-stay at position D1 and lead out to the opposite side of the table at position H. (If your dog isn't solid on his stay or if he lacks motivation, have a friend hold and restrain him to encourage a speedy performance.) Draw your dog's attention to the target and then call him to the obstacle using your command for the table. As he leaves the ground for the table, release him to the target with a command to *Get It*. The *Get It* cue marks the end of the exercise so your dog is not wrong if he comes off the table after eating the treat. It is a good idea, however, to encourage him to remain on the table by quickly approaching, petting, and praising him while he is on it. You might even give him an additional treat.

Gradually increase your dog's distance from the table (as shown by positions D2 through D5) until his starting position is 30' from the table. If successful, repeat the entire progression without using a target. Since you will not be releasing your dog with a *Get It* command, he must stay on the table (in any position) until you release him. When he jumps on the table, praise and pet him immediately and give him a treat from your hand. Then release with a release word or a command to *Come*. With added distance comes increased speed, so be prepared for the possibility that your dog may jump or slide off the table when no target is present. Since you are positioned close to the back side of the table, you can easily prevent him from sliding off.

Assuming you have mastered a snappy sit and down from a stand at a distance away from your agility training, you can then repeat the progression, adding the sit or down. Again, work without a target. However, this time issue a command for the desired position as your dog leaves the ground for the table. Since you are standing close to the back side of the table, you can immediately reinforce a quick response. Reward your dog in the correct position, then release and play.

Once your dog is performing brilliantly with you positioned close to the table, you can begin to increase your distance. Place your dog about 8' from table as shown in **Figure 5-3** and gradually increase your distance from the table as you call him to it (positions H1 through H5). Give your command to sit or down as he takes off for the obstacle. If successful, run up to the table and reward him in the assumed position. Then release and play. Then, increase your dog's speed to the table by gradually increasing his distance from the obstacle, as shown in **Figure 5-4.**

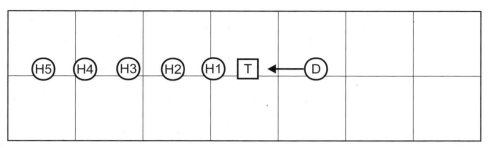

Figure 5-3

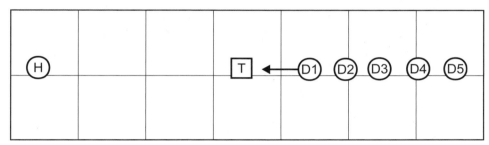

Figure 5-4

As your distance increases, your dog may become more likely to slide or jump off toward you. If this happens, give an immediate, unemotional verbal correction—such as *Wrong*—and then pick him up and place him back on the table. Follow with praise and petting. Take steps to prevent this mistake from happening on the next try. If you have a helper, you can station her near the table to prevent the dog from sliding off the table and to also have a reward nearby for timely reinforcement. Fade the helper by having her stand farther and farther away from the table. At some point your dog may slide off. If this happens, the helper (who is closer to the dog than the handler) can place the dog back on the table. On subsequent attempts, position the helper closer to help your dog be successful.

If you don't have a helper, you can place wire guides on the ground on the exit side of the table, as in **Figure 5-5**. Hopefully, the strange texture will surprise your dog when he lands on them, so he will work harder to remain on the table in the future. Yet another solution is to erect a temporary barrier around the three non-entrance sides of the table (jump wings or baby gates work well) to prevent your dog from leaving the table prematurely. Gradually fade the help.

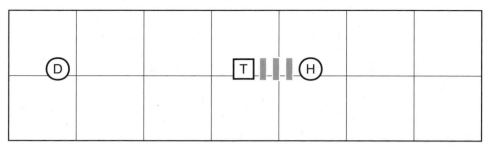

Figure 5-5

Train in different weather conditions and with a variety of table surfaces. This will teach your dog to hang on to the table at any speed, even if the table is slippery.

Sending to the Pause Table

Once you are successful at calling, start sending. It's important to practice sending both from an offset start and from your side. As you did when calling to the table, start with a target and a release to *Get It* for each exercise. Then repeat the progression without a target but also without a command to sit or down. Lastly, add the sit or down. If you have problems at any time, use an assistant, barriers, or wire guides as described above.

Offset Starts to the Table

When you send your dog to an obstacle using an offset start, you will leave your dog in a sit-stay and place yourself in a lateral handling position.

Start by positioning your dog as shown in **Figure 5-6**. Once again, if your dog is not absolutely solid on his stay or lacks motivation, disregard the stay and employ a friend to excite, restrain, and launch, if necessary. As always, speed is essential!

Lead out to position H1 as shown and face the dog's path, indicated by the X on the dog's path line. Extend your signaling arm (the arm closest to your dog) and face your body toward the X, then give your command for the table. If your dog is new to this exercise, it may help to take a few steps toward the X to help him establish the line you want him to take. When he catches on to the game, a single step forward toward the path marker will be all that he needs.

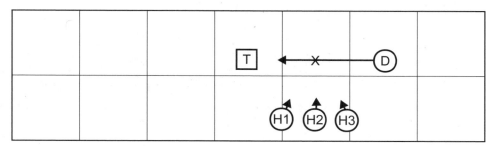

Figure 5-6

On subsequent tries, gradually decrease the amount of your lead-out (positions H2 and H3) to make the offset start more challenging. Gradually increase your lateral distance from your dog until you are successful working 30' to the side of him. Be sure to also work the mirror image of this exercise progression off your left.

Sending to the Table From Your Side

Your next goal is to be able to send your dog to the table from gradually increasing distances. Using the setup shown in **Figure 5-7** and facing parallel to your dog's path, gradually increase the distance from which you send your dog to the table. As you did earlier, start using a food-loaded target, release with a *Get It* cue, and do not ask for a sit or down. An assistant stationed near the table can help direct your dog's attention to the obstacle. Next, begin eliminating the target. Have your assistant encourage your dog to the table at first. Then, gradually eliminate the help. Once your dog is on the table, run up to meet him there and praise and reward him. Next, repeat the progression adding the sit or down.

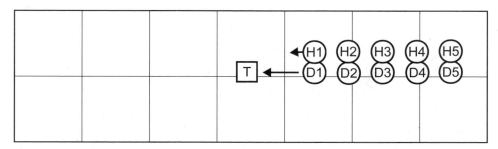

Figure 5-7

Be sure to also practice the mirror image of this exercise off your right.

RANDALL KNAPP

Chapter Six

Weave Poles at a Distance

There is nothing like the feeling of competing with a dog that can weave with breathtaking speed and utter precision—a dog that can find the most difficult entries and remain riveted to the task until the very last pole—regardless of your handling position on the course. Once you have achieved this level of teamwork with your dog, you will never again consider settling for anything less with the next dog you train.

If your dog insists that you run up and show him the correct entry and remain by his side as he weaves, you have inadvertently made yourself an integral part of your dog's weave-pole performance. When you try to vary your handling position, your dog most likely will not know how to perform his job.

On some courses, even the fastest handler can't get to the weave pole entry ahead of his dog without slowing the dog down or incurring a fault for a missed entry or refusal. Training your dog to enter and complete the poles at top speed and with total independence affords you the huge advantage of being able to send your dog ahead to weave while you position yourself optimally to handle the next series of obstacles. You are free to run ahead, hang back, or handle from a wide lateral position without sacrificing speed or accuracy.

The Importance of Head Position and Efficient Footwork

While it certainly is possible to train a dog that has poor head position and footwork while weaving to perform accurately at a distance, I would be remiss if I didn't *strongly* encourage you to assess your dog's skills and improve them, if necessary, before embarking on your weave-pole distance training. A dog that has mastered these skills will be *much* easier to train to weave at a distance. What's more, your performances will be *much* faster and more reliable; and training and competing will be more fun and rewarding for both you and your canine partner.

When your dog is weaving, you want his focus to be straight ahead—never looking toward the ground, from side to side, or upward toward you. Think about it. Could you run ahead at your fastest pace if you were looking anywhere other than straight ahead? Poor head position and focus also makes it more likely that your dog will get distracted and make a costly error.

For the most efficient path through the weave poles, you want your dog to use his muscles to actively hug the center line of the poles as closely as possible. A loose, meandering, S-shaped path or a wild, Z-shaped path will waste time and will make it more likely that your dog will miss a pole. The most efficient weave-pole footwork for your dog will largely be determined by his size and structure. For most large dogs (over 19"-20" at the withers) single-stepping is fastest and most efficient. The dog stretches forward and takes one long stride with alternating front legs between each pole, hugging the center line. Most smaller dogs will weave most efficiently by slaloming tightly along the center line of the poles with their two front legs moving together.

If you are already satisfied with your dog's weave-pole footwork and head position, read the section below entitled **What You Will Need.** This section describes the type of weave poles you will use to begin your weave-pole distance work. Then, skip ahead in this chapter to **Developing Distance Skills.** If you would like to improve your dog's weaving technique, however, continue ahead with the next section.

Retraining for Efficient Technique

The longer your dog has been weaving with a poor head position and/or footwork, the longer it will take you to retrain him. However, the time and effort will be well worth it as you reap the benefits of faster times, smoother runs, and more effective distance handling.

Retraining involves returning to basics—as if you were training your dog to weave for the first time. I highly recommend using my *FlashPaws Offset Weave Pole Method*. Dogs trained using this method are nationally known for their great speed, accuracy, and independence while weaving. Employing the principle of opposition reflex, the method uses motivational restraint to build drive and focus. Dogs learn to actively hug the center line of the poles and to expend all energy in a forward direction from the very start.

What You Will Need

Start with a set of 6 short weave poles offset 1-1/2" from a center line (or 3" from pole to pole) and spaced 20" apart. The poles themselves are 28" tall, rather than the typical 39" regulation poles so that you can lure your dog through the poles to encourage an efficient head position. The poles may be stuck in the ground or mounted in a base. It is preferable that the poles have some degree of flexibility to assist in developing the proper footwork and attitude from the start. If the base you are using is rigid, you can use flexible plastic electrical conduit instead of rigid PVC for the poles, as shown in **Figure 6-1**. You will also need at least 4 wire guides and a clip stick, as illustrated in ***Chapter 1: Tools and Concepts***.

Your goal is to build tremendous enthusiasm for weaving, so use only extra-special treats or toys for your training. Highly visible chunks of chicken, liver, cheese, and steak work well. For dogs that prefer toys, choose small, exciting toys that are only available to your dog during weave-pole training.

Although with very large dogs you can use your hand to hold the incentive while teaching your dog to weave, for most dogs I recommend using a clip stick instead. This will enable you to keep your posture upright, out of your dog's personal space. It will also make it easier to fade your incentive. If you don't have a clip stick, you can use an ordinary dowel dipped in peanut butter, liverwurst, or soft cheese.

Figure 6-1

Building Forward Drive

Before attempting the weave poles, teach your dog to pull toward the treat or toy on your stick. Place your dog on leash (small dogs) or a grab tab (large dogs) with a tight-fitting buckle collar. Hold the stick like a pencil, perpendicular to the ground with the incentive at your dog's eye level. Tease your dog with the treat and encourage him to pull toward it while you apply steady pressure at a 45-degree angle backward (never upward or forward!) using the leash or tab. When your dog is continuously pulling toward the stick without any slack in the leash, let him have his reward. Don't move on to the next step until your dog is elongating his neck and continuously pulling for the treat.

Introduction to the Offset Poles

Next, you can progress to the set of 6 short, offset poles. With your dog on leash, encourage him to pull toward the treat on the stick as you did before. When he is pulling continuously and there is no slack in the leash, give your command to *Weave* and approach the poles head-on. Lure your dog straight through the center of the poles using verbal encouragement and by enticing him with the treat directly in front of his nose as shown in **Figure 6-2**. Face the direction your dog is going; do not walk backwards or sideways! This enables you to move ahead quickly and will help ease the transition as you fade the use of the incentive.

Figure 6-2

To encourage efficient footwork, prevent your dog from taking a wild Z-shaped or loose S-shaped path through the poles. You can help achieve this by moving the clip stick with only a slight, controlled movement of your wrist (rather than a dramatic zigzag motion) and by keeping your leash taut. As your dog catches on, begin to hold the incentive farther away from his nose, until it remains one or more poles ahead of him the entire time that he is weaving.

Make sure that you bring your luring arm completely and smoothly over the top of the poles so that you are not raising and lowering your treat as the dog weaves. (Make a "U" shape around your armpit—do not clench your upper arm to your body.) Keep your dog driving forward and focused ahead at all times. If he looks down at the ground, away to the side, or up at you, bring the incentive closer to his nose to regain his forward attention and then resume weaving. Give him his reward and praise profusely as he exits.

Be sure to work this and all stages of your weave-pole training equally off your right and your left. Whichever side you are working on, hold your leash in the hand closest to your dog and your stick in the opposite hand.

Using Wire Guides

The use of wire guides will be *essential* for training your dog to enter and complete the poles at full speed regardless of your handling position. Now is the best time to introduce them—while your dog is focusing on the reward at the end of the clip stick. Start by placing two guides at the weave-pole entrance to help him enter correctly, as shown in **Figure 6-3**.

Figure 6-3

The first time you use wire guides, some dogs display initial avoidance. Others plow them down or jump over them without a care. Through patience and repetition you can show your dog there is nothing to fear. You can teach him not to jump over the wire by guiding him through the poles with a huge incentive on your stick at eye level. If he jumps the wire, prevent him from repeating the mistake on the next try by holding his collar or tab and praising him continuously as he passes the guide. He will soon catch on. For dogs that continue to jump over the guides, use extra-high ones. Eventually you can transition to the lower guides.

Eliminating the Leash

When you can hold your incentive at least one pole ahead of your dog while maintaining correct head position, drive, and accuracy; you are ready to try eliminating the leash or tab.

Remove his leash and transfer the stick to the hand closest to your dog. Place him in a sit-stay (only if it is rock-solid stay!) or have a friend hold him about 2' from the weave-pole entry. Position your stick between the first and second pole so that you can get a head start and remain at least one pole ahead of your dog the entire time that he is weaving. Give your command to *Weave* and have your dog follow the incentive straight through the center of the poles. If there is a particular pole or two that your dog tries to skip, strategically placed wire guides can help him be successful.

Gradually position the stick farther and farther ahead of your dog while he is weaving. When you notice that he appears to be doing his job well without focusing on the stick, you can begin to fade the use of it.

If you would like additional help on weave-pole foundation skills, this subject covered in much greater detail in ***Excelling at Dog Agility— Book 1: Obstacle Training and Competitive Agility Training with Jane Simmons-Moake—DVD 1: Obstacle Training.***

Developing Distance Skills

To develop distance skills on the weave poles, it is necessary to be able to call and send your dog to the poles. Your dog must also be able do his job with speed and accuracy regardless of any movements you make or any distractions that are present.

IMPORTANT NOTE: The figures in this chapter show all of the exercises using 6 regulation (in-line) poles. Keep in mind, however, that the ideal progression is to begin all exercises with 6 offset poles. Then, repeat the entire set of exercises with 12 offset poles, then with 6 regulation poles, then eventually with 12 regulation poles.

Calling to the Weave Poles

The first step in developing weaving independence is to call your dog through the weave poles from a variety of angles and distances. When weaving toward you, your dog will be motivated to work quickly and confidently.

Position two wire guides at the entrance to make it easy for your dog to enter the poles correctly. Place your dog in a sit-stay about 12" from the correct entrance to the poles. Alternatively, you may wish to have an assistant hold your dog in position and release him when you give your command.

Place your right foot against the left side of the base of the weave poles at about the fourth pole as shown in **Figure 6-4**. Place your left foot as far behind you as possible. (Make sure both of your feet are facing parallel to the weave-pole base.) Shift your weight to your right foot, Hold a treat or toy in your right hand or attached to a clip stick at the dog's nose level (to encourage optimal head position). Give your command to *Weave*, shift your weight to your back foot and take a long step back with your right foot as you lure your dog through the poles with the incentive.

Entice your dog straight through the weave-pole channel. Do not use a zigzag motion when luring your dog through the poles. Keep the incentive steady at the dog's nose level. Don't allow your hand to move up and down as your arm moves over the top of the poles. You want to keep the height of the lure steady to help encourage a consistent head position. Praise and reward him as he exits the last pole. Gradually increase the distance you lead out until you can call your dog through the entire set of poles (**Figure 6-5**).

Figure 6-4

Figure 6-5

Continue your training using the setup shown in **Figure 6-6**. Place your dog in a sit-stay at position D1 and lead out to the opposite side of the weave poles at position H. (If your dog isn't rock-solid on his stay or if he lacks motivation, have a friend hold and restrain him.) Call him through the weave poles with an enthusiastic command to *Weave*. If all goes well, vary your dog's starting position with each successive attempt (positions D2 though D7).

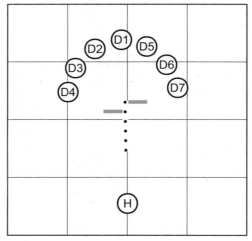

Figure 6-6

If your dog makes a mistake, mark the moment of the error with an unemotional verbal correction such as *Wrong*. Then, make it easier to succeed on the next attempt by using additional wire guides.

Next, train your dog to exit correctly regardless of your handling position as shown in **Figure 6-7**. Position guides at the exit to ensure your dog will not anticipate his reward and exit prematurely. Begin at position H1 and gradually progress through positions H2 through H7. Remember to give a signal using the hand closest to your dog, and to face the "path"—a point midway between your dog's current position and the obstacle.

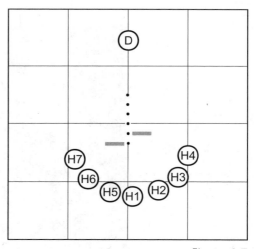

Figure 6-7

Next, vary both your dog's starting position and your handling position as shown in **Figure 6-8**. Begin using position H1/D1, then progress to H2/D2, and so forth. Remember, when the entry angles become more extreme, it is very important to face your body and signal toward the path—not toward the obstacle.

Once you are successful, begin to increase your distance and your dog's distance from the poles. Work gradually until both you and your dog are 30' from the poles **(Figure 6-9).** As your dog approaches from farther away, his speed will be greater and nailing the correct entry will be more of a challenge. Using guides for the entry will ensure that your dog is successful without micromanagement from you. Eventually remove the guides, one at a time, until he is successful without any help.

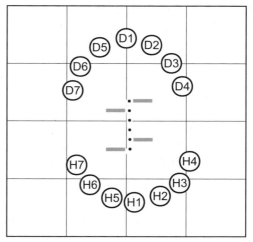

Figure 6-8

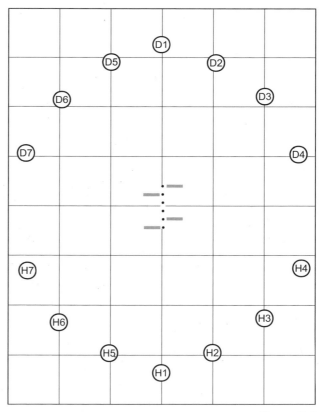

Figure 6-9

Sending to the Weave Poles

When—and only when—you are successful at calling through the poles, begin sending. All of your previous work with calling through the poles will give your dog the confidence and independence he needs to be successful with sending. As you did with the other obstacles, you will send your dog from your side and from an offset start.

Sending From Your Side

When sending through the poles it is helpful to place a reward for your dog on the exit end of the weave poles. In doing so, you will condition your dog to continue ahead after exiting, rather than curling back to you for his reward. A good way to accomplish this (and to discourage cheating) is to position a pause table about 3' from the exit and place a food-loaded target or a favorite toy on the back side of a table (**Figure 6-10**). This will also keep your dog focused straight ahead instead of toward the ground.

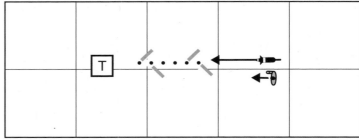

Position wire guides at the entry and exit of the weave poles to help ensure success. Command and signal him to

Figure 6-10

Weave and start moving toward the poles, facing parallel to the path you want him to take. Once your dog has entered correctly, begin to smoothly and gradually hang back and allow him to finish the last two or three poles on his own. The moment his nose passes the last pole, give your *Table* command. As soon as your dog leaves the ground for the table, release him to the target with a command to *Get It*. The *Get It* is a release from working so don't ask for a sit or down. Each time you repeat the exercise, gradually hang back more and more until your dog is weaving through the entire set with you remaining behind all of the poles. You should be able to send him off either your right or left side.

Gradually increase the entry angle, being sure to face parallel to the path you want your dog to take, as shown in **Figures 6-11 through 6-13**.

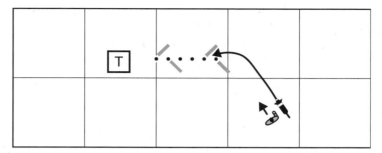

Figure 6-11

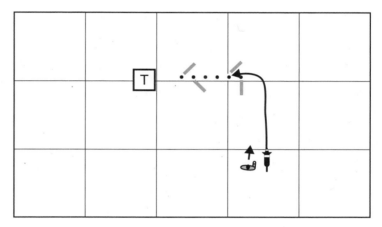

Figure 6-12

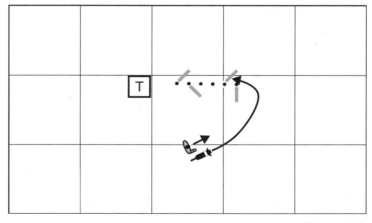

Figure 6-13

Offset Starts to the Weave Poles

When you send your dog to the weave poles using an offset start, you will leave your dog in a sit-stay and place yourself in a lateral handling position.

Start by positioning your dog as shown in **Figure 6-14**. Once again, if your dog is not absolutely solid on his stay or lacks motivation, disregard the stay and employ a friend to excite, restrain, and launch, if necessary. Lead out to position H1 as shown and face the dog's path, indicated by the X on the dog's path line. Extend your signaling arm (the arm closest to your dog) and face your body toward the X, then give your command for the weave poles. If your dog is new to this exercise, it may help to take a few steps toward the X to help him establish the line you want him to take. When he catches on to the game, a single step forward toward the path will be all that is needed.

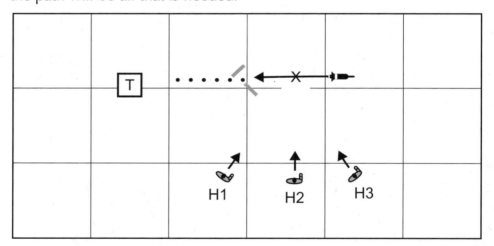

Figure 6-14

On subsequent tries, gradually decrease the amount of your lead-out (positions H2 and H3) to make the offset start more challenging. Gradually increase your lateral distance from your dog until you are successful working 30' to the side of him. Be sure to also work the mirror image of this exercise progression off your left.

Next, increase your dog's angle of approach to the weave poles and follow the progressions shown in **Figures 6-15 and 6-16**. Eventually remove the wire guides until your dog is performing at top speed and flawlessly without help from the guides.

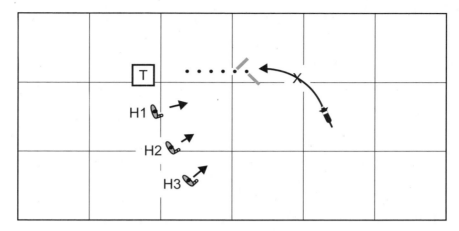

Figure 6-15

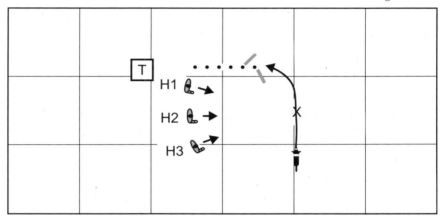

Proofing for Reliability

Figure 6-16

Now that your dog is weaving with speed and accuracy, regardless of your handling position, it's time to train him to be just as fast and accurate regardless of any distractions that may be present. In the ring those distractions might include movements by the handler such as racing ahead, pulling away—even falling down! Other distractions might include sudden noises, cheering, or toys and food outside the ring.

One reason many dogs make weave-pole errors in competition is that they have not been trained to tune out all distractions and focus on their weaving. You can accomplish this by gradually incorporating distractions into your training. While this may sound scary at first to some people, distraction proofing is quite fun for both dog and handler. Besides developing reliability, most dogs weave even faster as a result.

Your goal should be to build confidence and to reward success with very high-value rewards. To help maintain good footwork and to help promote early success, it's best to start with 6 offset poles.

The distractions you use should be very mild at first. A person walking nearby or a distracting object placed on the ground several feet away can be enough to take your dog's concentration from his work. If he makes a mistake, at the precise moment of his infraction give your non-emotional verbal correction such as *Wrong, Oops,* or *Uh-Oh.* Repeat immediately, making it easier for the dog to succeed. To do this, you might make the distracting person remain farther away, move the distracting object farther from view, or position wire guides at the position(s) in the poles where your dog is likely to become distracted.

As your dog catches on to the game, gradually increase the level of distraction. Some dogs will be able to progress quite quickly to large distractions. More tentative dogs may need several weeks of gradually increasing distractions. Use your imagination to come up with interesting distractions. All is fair except things that might frighten or injure the dog. Suggestions include:

♦ Handler movements such as running ahead, pulling away, flailing signals, spinning around—and my personal favorite—running in the opposite direction while your dog is weaving.

♦ Movement of other people and nearby dogs.

♦ Squeaky toys, balls, and other toys. Start by placing one nearby, then place it closer, then drop it, then throw it.

♦ Food in containers (that the dog cannot self-reward with).

♦ Music, cheering, whistles, clapping and any other interesting sounds you can come up with. Two of my favorite sound distractions are the rattling of a potato-chip bag and a "squirrel call" purchased from a sporting goods store.

It is also important to occasionally position your weave poles to exit close to the end or corner of your training area or close to a ring barrier. Your dog must learn to complete all of the poles without being distracted by the barrier and without anticipating an upcoming turn.

Once you are successful with 6 offset poles, progress to 12 offsets, then 6 regular poles, and finally 12 or more regular poles.

Chapter Seven

Sequencing Using Lateral Distance

Through the work you have done in the previous chapters you have mastered each of the individual agility obstacles at a wide variety of angles and at distances of up to 30' away from you. Your dog should now be able to attack the entry and neatly exit each obstacle on his own with accuracy and confidence—and all at his fastest speed. These newfound skills are the essential building blocks you will use to execute smooth, fast, and accurate sequences at a distance.

Having the ability to handle a sequence at a distance can often be a great advantage. In **Figure 7-1**, the handler's ability to handle wide allows him to be in an advantageous position to push to the path to facilitate the weave pole entry. As a result, he completes the sequence smoothly and quickly. The handler who cannot work at a distance for obstacles #1 through #3 may find himself in a poor position to handle obstacle #4 as in **Figure 7-2**.

On any given course you can find areas where it would be advantageous to handle at a distance, particularly if you have a fast dog. Handlers with speedy canine partners fully understand the benefits of being able to send the dog ahead to complete a sequence while they move into position to handle a control point elsewhere on the course. By taking a shorter path than your dog and handling at a wide lateral distance, you can smoothly communicate the course while your dog runs at full speed.

Figure 7-3 shows one of the simplest yet most useful exercises for building lateral distance. When you encounter this common sequence on a course, it is often to your advantage to be able to handle it from behind jumps #1 and #3. This provides you the flexibility of getting ahead for the next series of obstacles while letting your dog fly through the sequence.

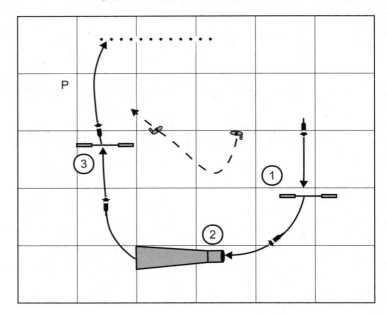

Figure 7-1

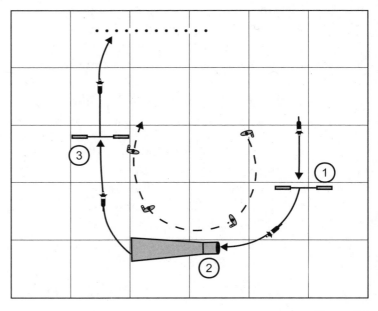

Figure 7-2

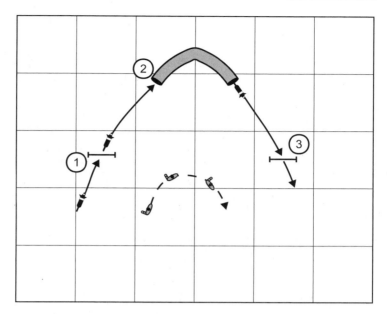

Figure 7-3

Because your dog has already mastered calling and sending to tunnels and jumps, including offset starts (lateral lead-outs), you have all the skills necessary to ace this sequence at a distance.

To help ensure success, it helps to backchain the sequence as shown in **Figure 7-4**. Backchaining refers to teaching a performance starting with the last part and then gradually working backward toward the starting point. Backchaining builds confidence and early success since the dog is always working toward a familiar endpoint.

Notice that the obstacles are only spaced about 15' apart. Beginning with closely-spaced sequences also helps build early success.

How to Begin

First, place your dog at the exit end of the tunnel and send him to the last jump using an offset start. Give your command and signal for the jump, facing path marker P (midway between the dog's current location and the next obstacle you want him to take). If successful, set your dog up as shown in **Figure 7-5** and begin with an offset start to the tunnel (facing path marker P1), followed by the jump (facing P2).

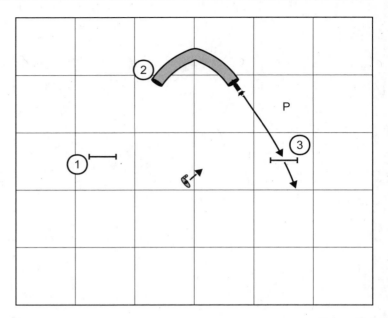

Figure 7-4

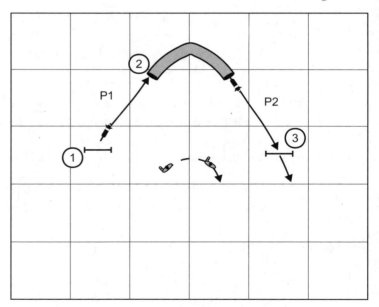

Figure 7-5

Finally, start with jump #1 as shown in **Figure 7-6**. Be sure to face and signal toward each of the path markers as you complete the sequence. Keep your signals and body movements continuous, smooth, and fluid. It may help to imagine that you are handling in a "vat of molasses." Sudden jerky movements and abruptly dropped signals may cause your dog to check back with you or pull off an obstacle.

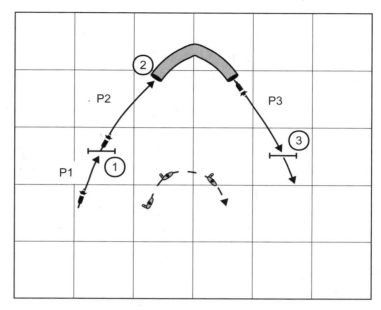

Figure 7-6

If You Have Problems

If at any time your dog pulls off an obstacle, freeze and look down at your feet. Are they facing the path (between your dog's current position and the next obstacle)? The direction your feet are facing is usually a good indicator of the body cue you are giving to your dog. People often find that they have over-turned. In our classes, we use physical path markers such as the smiley face on a stand shown in **Figure 7-7**. These strategically placed markers help provide a visible reminder for handlers.

If, despite facing the correct direction and handling smoothly, you still have problems, take steps to ensure success on the next try by doing one or more of the following:

♦ Return to backchaining at the last successful sequence, using a target, if necessary.

♦ Handle somewhat closer (and then gradually increase your distance after each successful attempt).

How to Progress

Perform the mirror image of the exercise progression off your right. Then, gradually increase the spacing between obstacles until they are 30' apart, as in **Figure 7-8**. Once you've mastered this, make a mental note about how good this feels and how much fun it is for both you and your dog! Many people attain success at this stage, are pleasantly surprised by their accomplishment, and then revert to their old Velcro-handling ways in their day-to-day training. If you want to feel confident in choosing a distance handling strategy at a trial, you must put these skills into practice on a regular basis. Your goal is to make distance work business-as-usual for both you and your dog.

Figure 7-7

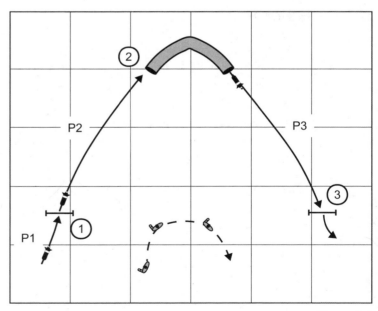

Figure 7-8

IMPORTANT NOTE: Successful distance handling is never lazy handling. It is not loose, cavalier, or unmotivated handling. Your motions should all possess smooth fluidity. At the same time, however, both your commands and body movements should also display intensity, accuracy, confidence, and a sense of urgency. For the best handlers, distance work is not a leisurely stroll in the park; it is an exciting race against the stopwatch—a chance to top your personal best!

Setting up Additional Exercises

Once you are successful with the jump-tunnel-jump sequence, set up similar three-obstacle sequences in an arced configuration. The arc-shaped sequences help make it easy to be successful. It is also a very common configuration encountered on courses.

Remember to include in your sequences only obstacles that you have mastered individually at a distance. As with the first exercise, start with 15' spacing between obstacles and then backchain the sequence. Then, gradually increase the spacing between obstacles until they are 30' apart. If the sequences are bi-directional (i.e., they contain no seesaws or chutes,) practice the exercises off both your right and your left sides by reversing direction.

Some suggestions for sequences are shown in **Figures 7-9 through 7-13**. These examples all show the final goal sequence using 30' spacing.

Your goal is to instill confidence in working at a distance and that confidence comes from success. If you repeatedly need to stop your sequencing to work through missed contacts or missed poles, you may be defeating your goal of building a positive attitude toward distance work. When sequences include contact obstacles it is a good idea to position wire guides adjacent to the up ramps to ensure a straight approach. You may also want to consider using targets or other aids to assist with the performance of the downside contact. Likewise, when including weave poles in your sequences, you may want to position guides at the entry and/or exit to help ensure success from the start. Once you are successful using the wire guides and/or target, you can gradually remove them.

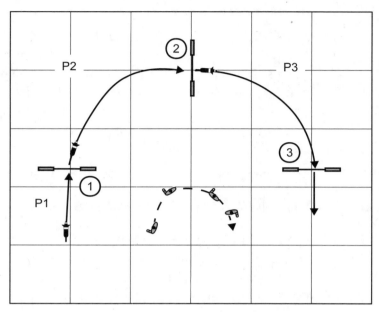

Figure 7-9

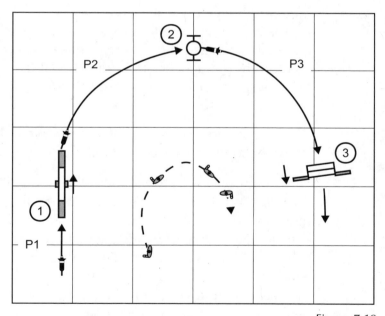

Figure 7-10

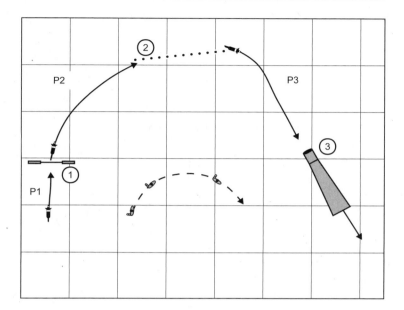

Figure 7-11

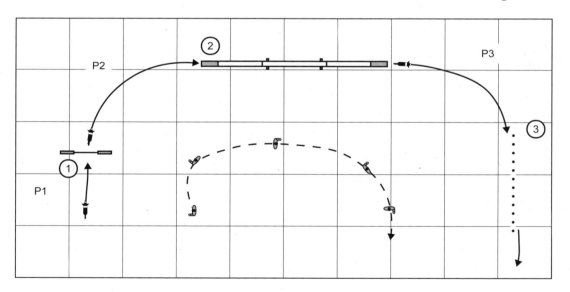

Figure 7-12

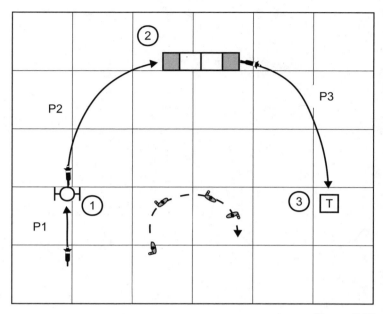

Figure 7-13

Chapter Eight

Learning to Love Layering

There will be many times on an agility course when you will want to keep one or more obstacles between you and your dog while sequencing. This valuable skill is referred to as *layering*. The ability to layer can be necessary when obstacles are positioned close together, as in the #6-#7-#8 and the #17-#18-#19 sequences in the course example shown in **Figure 8-1**.

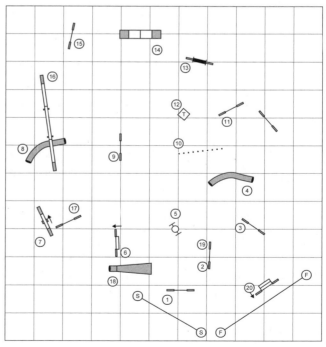

Figure 8-1

Layering can also be extremely advantageous when handling "box" sequences. Consider the box of jumps formed by jumps #4, #5, A, and B in **Figure 8-2**. If you run inside the box to handle jumps #1 through #5, you risk pushing your dog away from you over incorrect jump B.

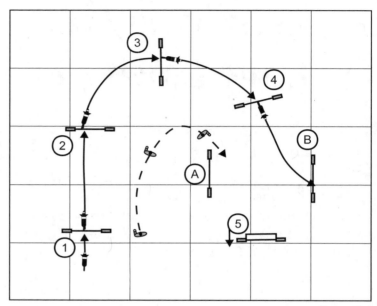

Figure 8-2

If instead you handled from outside the box, as shown in **Figure 8-3**, your dog would be likely to continue smoothly and confidently to jump #5.

To understand why this works, examine the situation from your dog's point of view. With your dog's angle of approach from jump #4, the first obstacle he sees is jump B. Without a cue to turn, he is likely to continue ahead to the incorrect jump.

To signal a gentle right turn to jump #5, you must rotate your shoulders clockwise (parallel to the path you want him to take) as your dog takes off for jump #4. If you are running forward to get inside the box at the same time your dog is jumping #4, as shown in Figure 8-2, your body is not signaling a turn. Instead, you are clearly indicating with your body language that you want him to continue straight ahead and take jump B. The longer you have been training agility the more you will realize that when your body cues and verbal commands conflict, the vast majority of dogs will follow your body language.

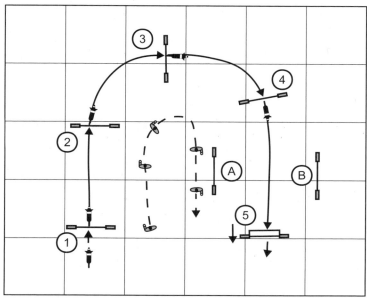

Figure 8-3

The thought of layering strikes fear in the hearts of many new agility handlers. Their biggest fear is that the dog will take the obstacle they are layering, rather than the correct one. If the maneuver is executed correctly, this rarely happens because the layered obstacle is usually the last obstacle the dog sees. This can happen, however, if the handler runs inside a line made by the obstacle to be layered, and then pulls out, pulling the dog with him, as shown in **Figure 8-4**. You can avoid this by planning your handling path to remain behind the line made by jump A. You will then be free to give a timely body cue to turn when your dog commits to jump #4. The result is a smooth and gentle turn to jump #5.

How to Begin

The first step in your layering training is to work with closely spaced pairs of obstacles, such as the seesaw and tunnel arrangement shown in **Figure 8-5**. To start, choose the tunnel as the outside obstacle and position the high end of the seesaw adjacent to the tunnel opening. This setup will accustom your dog to working with an obstacle between you and him, while making it easy to be successful.

Position your dog and yourself as shown. Face your feet and shoulders midway between the dog and the tunnel, as indicated by path marker P. Fully

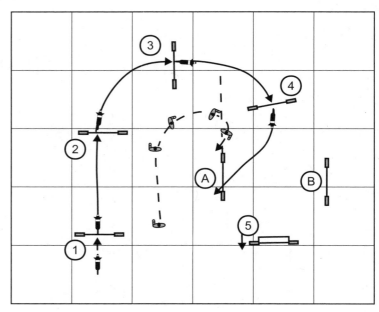

Figure 8-4

extend your signaling arm (the arm closest to your dog) toward P, give an enthusiastic command for the tunnel, and then take small steps forward toward the path marker without crossing an imaginary line made by the edge of the seesaw. Be careful not to face the tunnel opening, and be sure to give your command before you start moving. Praise and reward your dog as he exits the tunnel.

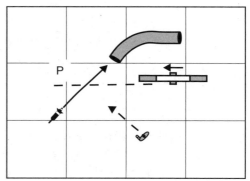

Figure 8-5

If successful, turn the seesaw around so that your dog has a choice of taking the tunnel or the seesaw, as shown in **Figure 8-6**.

Once you are successful sending to the tunnel, ask for the seesaw on a subsequent try, as shown in **Figure 8-7**. As before, position your dog in a direct line with the tunnel. Start with your signaling arm straight down at your side, give your *Come* command, followed by your command for the seesaw, as soon as your dog sees it. At the same time, give your body cue for the turn to the seesaw, (which is to face your entire body

parallel to the obstacle toward path marker P) while smoothly extending your signaling arm straight ahead, keeping your upper arm close to
your body.

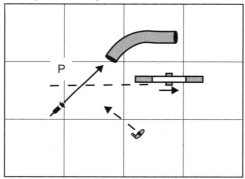

| *Figure 8-6* | *Figure 8-7* |

If your dog is successful, randomly alternate between directing your dog
to the inside choice versus the outside choice. This will help reinforce
your dog's understanding of the cues you will use for each option.

NOTE: *When asking your dog to take the inside choice, you should travel
a path that is parallel to the path you want your dog to take. When asking for the outside choice, you should face the dog's path, which is most
often halfway between the dog's current position and the next obstacle
you want him to take.*

If You Have Problems

Your dog may have taken an incorrect obstacle. This can happen if you
face the obstacle itself rather than the path (for the tunnel) or parallel to
the path (for the seesaw).

This can also occur if you neglect to stay completely behind the seesaw
boundary (dashed line in Figures 8-5 through 8-7). This causes you to get
caught behind the layered obstacle. To continue ahead, you must turn
away from the correct path, which pulls your dog away with (toward)
you. Staying behind the seesaw boundary keeps your path smooth and
helps keep your dog on track.

For dogs that continue to have trouble despite good handling, try blocking the incorrect choice with a barrier such as a wire guide, jump wing, or baby gate. Alternatively, you could target the correct obstacle with food or a toy as an incentive. Give high-value rewards for success, and gradually eliminate the extra help.

How to Progress

When your dog is doing well at this stage, gradually add more distance between the obstacles as shown in **Figure 8-8**.

You can also add obstacles before and after the layered pair as shown in **Figures 8-9 and 8-10**. As you direct your dog, be sure to face the path markers for each option.

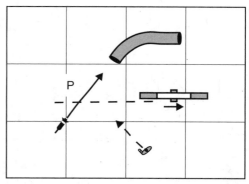

Figure 8-8

Next, try layering with many different pairs of obstacles. Then, add distance and then add additional obstacles before and after the layered pair. Include only obstacles that you have mastered at a distance. If you cannot guarantee speed and accuracy at a distance on an individual obstacle, revisit one of the earlier chapters in this book and master these skills before layering with that obstacle.

Another sample layering exercise progression is shown in **Figures 8-11 through 8-14**. As with every exercise, if your dog makes a mistake, stop right away. Then, isolate and work through the problem before continuing on.

The more layering becomes comfortable for you and business-as-usual for you and your dog, the more you will enjoy choosing and using this valuable handling strategy.

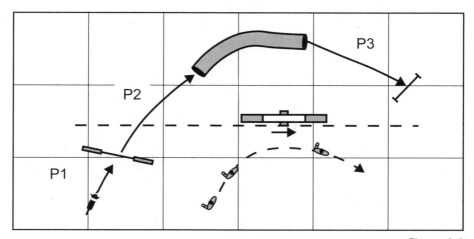

Figure 8-9

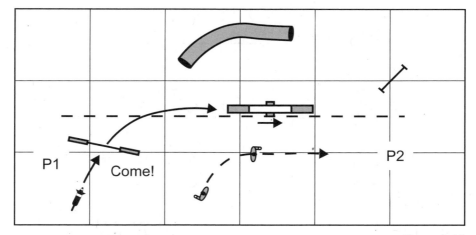

Figure 8-10

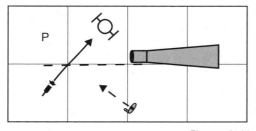

Figure 8-11

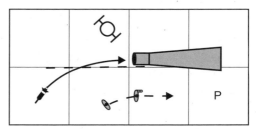

Figure 8-12

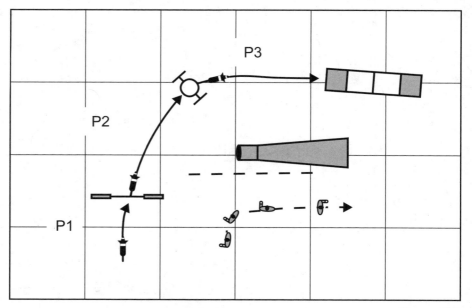

Figure 8-13

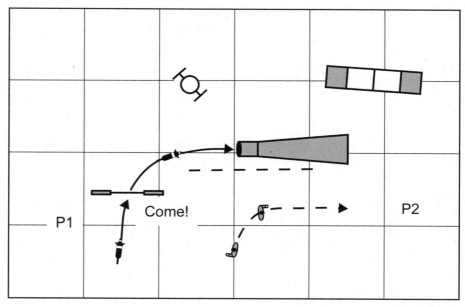

Figure 8-14

Chapter Nine

Lateral Distance Through Circle Training

The ability to direct your dog through sequences at a lateral distance is essential to have in your agility handling toolbox. Handing "wide" allows you to take a shorter path than your dog, so that you can take advantage of your dog's fastest speed as you strategically position yourself ahead on the course. This ability is especially important if you have a fast dog and/or if you are not the world's fastest handler.

A great exercise for building lateral distance is the distance circle. Directing your dog through circles is a bit like driving a fast car on a racetrack! You and your dog will both have a great time while building confidence and speed at a distance.

Prerequisites

Before attempting distance circles, you should be able to send your dog on one command and signal to each obstacle in the circle from your side and from an offset start (lateral lead-out) from a distance of up to 30'. If your dog has not mastered these skills, revisit the earlier chapters of this book.

Overview

Your goal is to be able to direct your dog to perform a circle of obstacles while you handle from the center of the circle. Eventually you should be able to start with any obstacle on the circle and end with any obstacle.

You should be able to start the exercise by sending your dog to the first obstacle from your side at the center of the circle. You should alternatively be able to start by positioning him in front of the first obstacle and directing him from an offset start position.

To make it easy for your dog to be successful, it is a good idea to begin your training by using the tunnel as your first obstacle (rather than a jump) and by sending your dog from your side (rather than using an offset start).

Mastering the Distance Circle

Arrange a small circle of jumps and tunnels as shown in **Figure 9-1**. Since you will be sending your dog from your side, your starting position will be facing parallel to your dog's path to the first obstacle. Complete the entire circle, running as close as you feel necessary to get the job done smoothly.

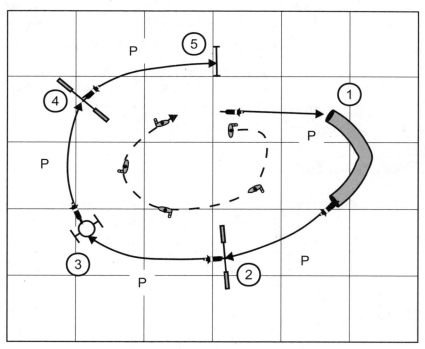

Figure 9-1

At any given point in the sequence, you want your shoulders and signaling hand to be facing the path, midway between where your dog is and the next obstacle you want him to take. For example, when he leaves the tunnel you want to be facing between the tunnel exit and the next jump while giving your *Jump* command.

Concentrate on your command timing. Give your command for the jump before your dog's head exits the tunnel. Give your command for the tire as your dog takes off for the jump that precedes it, and so on. If your dog head-checks you between obstacles, it is a good indication that your commands are late.

Many handlers trying this exercise for the first time will have a tendency to take a huge step toward the path marker and freeze. You will have much better results if you keep moving, even if you are only taking small steps. Dogs have excellent peripheral vision, and they can see and sense your movement even when you are behind them. If you stop moving, you are no longer giving information to your dog. As result, he may stop or lose momentum, and check back with you.

As you are moving, remember to keep your shoulders and signal square to the path markers between each obstacle. From the dog's point of view, this makes it clear where you want him to go.

Once successful, gradually increase your lateral distance on subsequent attempts until you are eventually occupying only a small circle at the center of the obstacles as shown in **Figure 9-2**. Be sure to work all sequences off both your right and your left.

When you have mastered this exercise, repeat the progression beginning with an offset start as shown in **Figures 9-3 and 9-4**. When beginning with an offset start, your starting position will be facing your dog's path indicated by P—not parallel to the path as you did when previously sending from your side.

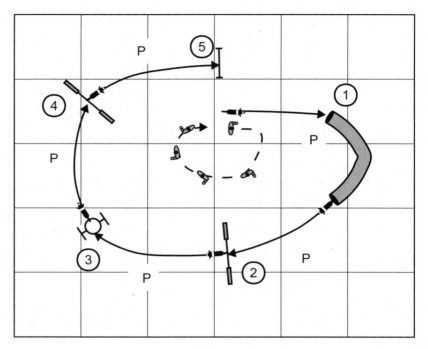

Figure 9-2

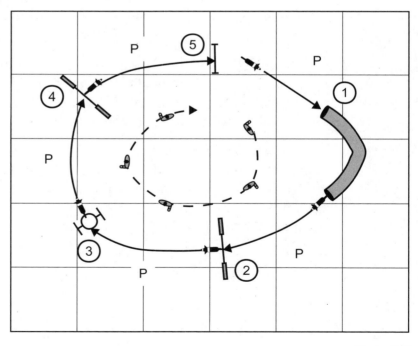

Figure 9-3

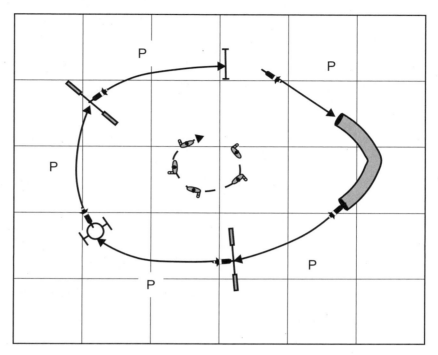

Figure 9-4

If You Have Problems

If at any time you experience a problem, stop and deal with it right away by isolating the problem (performing only a two-obstacle sequence) and making it easier to be successful (by handling closer and/or by using training aids such as wire guides or targets).

Your dog may have run past an obstacle as in **Figure 9-5**. This can happen if you face the next obstacle rather than the desired path. From the dog's point of view, it appears that you want him to skip the next obstacle. Try the exercise again, this time trying to focus on the space between the obstacles—not the obstacles themselves. The more you work at a lateral distance the more this will become second nature to you as a handler.

Another reason your dog may bypass an obstacle is if you get too close to an obstacle and then start to pull away in an effort to return to the center of the circle. Pulling away with your body will pull your dog away with you. To prevent this on subsequent attempts, draw a circle on the ground to remind you of your handling boundaries.

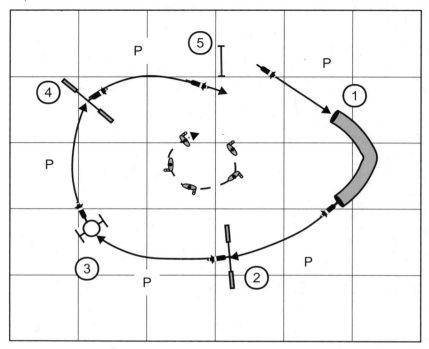

Figure 9-5

If your dog bypasses an obstacle and you're not sure of the reason, freeze and look at the direction your body is facing (arm, shoulders, and feet). All parts of your body should be facing the path—between the dog's current position and the next obstacle you want him to take. Errors often occur when you are not facing the path, or when your body parts are facing in different directions.

If your signaling arm faces the path and your shoulders and feet are facing the obstacle, you are giving an ambiguous cue. Your dog will need to decide for himself what you are indicating. If you are not sure of the cause of the error, assume that you were to blame. Repeat the sequence, concentrating on your handling.

How to Progress

Next, start the circles with obstacles other than the tunnel. Then, start inserting random call-offs. As much as you want your dog to enjoy soaring around the ring at a distance, it is equally important to be able to reel him in at will. Ask your dog to fly around the circle once or twice, then surprise him with a command and simultaneous body cue to *Come*. Make sure your body cue is not facing the path to the next obstacle when you issue your command to *Come*. If you do, your body cue is likely to override your verbal command in your dog's eyes.

Once you have mastered sequencing on this circle, gradually increase its size as in **Figure 9-6**. Then add more difficult obstacles, such as contacts and weave poles as shown in **Figure 9-7**. You can use wire guides with the weave poles and contact obstacles to prevent your dog from making entry mistakes while you are working on increasing distance. Once successful, you can fade the use of the guides.

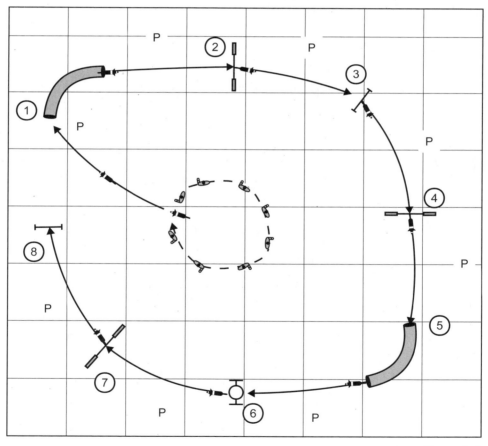

Figure 9-6

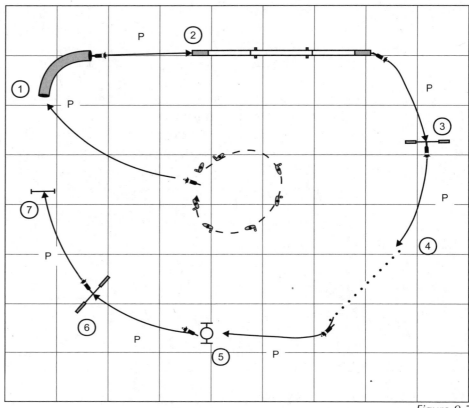

Figure 9-7

Progress to performing the same circle beginning with an offset start as shown in **Figure 9-8.**

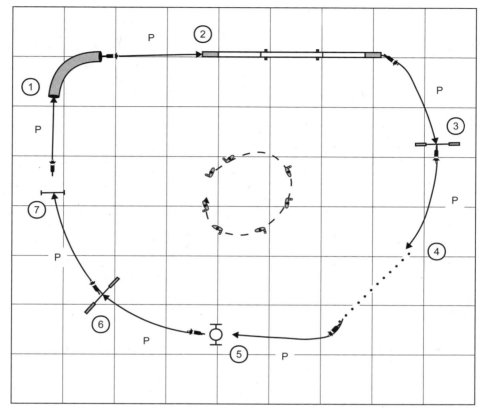

Figure 9-8

Concentric Circles

Next begins the real fun—working with concentric circles. With an inner circle and an outer circle, you can strengthen your lateral distance skills as well as your layering skills.

First, direct your dog through the inner circle. You can begin the circle from your side or from an offset start as shown in **Figure 9-9**. Once you're successful, direct your dog through the outer circle, beginning with an offset start as in **Figure 9-10**. The dog should not cut in toward you but follow a parallel path to your signal and remain on the outer circle.

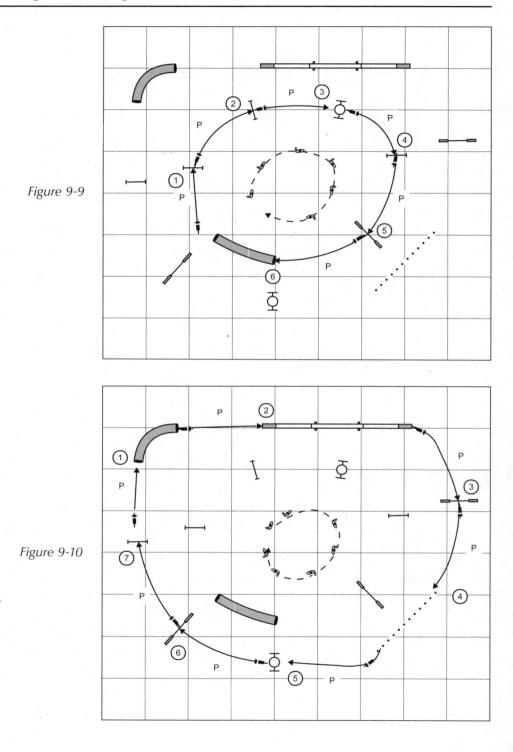

Figure 9-9

Figure 9-10

Chapter Ten

Lateral Pushing Using the *Out* Command

B efore extolling the virtues of the *Out* command, let's define the behavior. Simply put, *Out* is a directional change that means "turn away from the handler." For example, when you are handling off your left, saying *Come* (or *Here*) pulls the dog to his right while commanding *Out* pushes the dog to his left.

I sometimes observe people issuing the command *Out* when they do not want a directional turn—they only want the dog to continue straight ahead without a turn. If you use *Out* in this way, you will need to choose a different command (for example, *Back*) for a lateral push. It will confuse your dog if you use the same command for two completely different behaviors.

The *Out* command is indispensable for distance training and handling. It affords you the enormous benefit of being able to push your dog out laterally while you take a shortcut on the course. This enables you to take full advantage of your dog's maximum speed while allowing you to move freely to a strategic handling position for an upcoming sequence as in **Figure 10-1**. What's more, when layering, you can use the *Out* command to push your dog to the outside layer, while you continue on an inside path as in **Figure 10-2**. Once mastered, it is very likely that you will decide that *Out* is one of the most useful commands in your distance-handling toolbox.

Figure 10-1

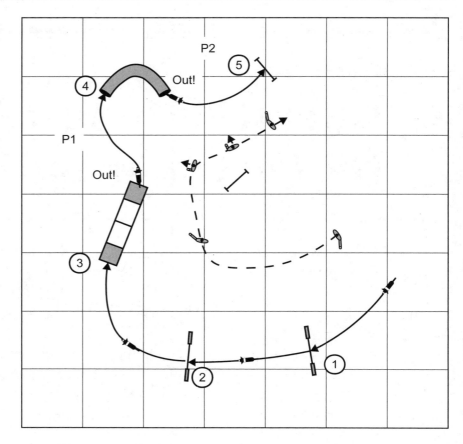

Figure 10-2

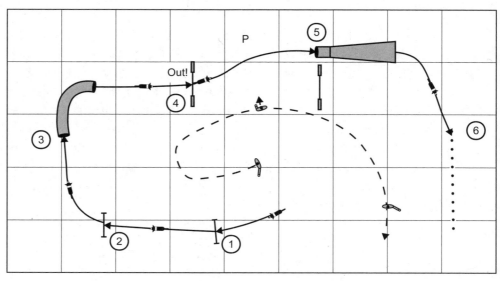

How the Out Command Works

When you want an outward turn after a jump you give your *Out* command as your dog commits to the jump. For an outward turn after tunnels, contact obstacles, or weave poles, you give your *Out* command as he completes the obstacle. At the same time you will square your shoulders and give a flat-palm signal facing the path you want your dog to take. Through earlier chapters in this book you are now quite familiar with the concept of "facing the path." This means facing a point that is generally midway between the dog's current position and the next obstacle you want him to take. Once your dog has turned outward and can see the next obstacle, you will give your obstacle command.

Handler Positions and the Out Command

A wonderful aspect of the *Out* command and body cue is that it works regardless of your distance from your dog. Consider the many body cues you may currently be giving to your dog. While all of these cues can communicate your wishes when you are working close to your dog, try them while you are 25'-35' or more from the correct obstacle. Try them also when there is a layered obstacle between you and your dog. You may discover that your dog has no idea where to go. To see why this is true, observe the situation from your dog's point of view while a friend gives you these cues at a distance.

Unlike many cues that break down once the handler is far from the next obstacle, the *Out* command/signal cues work at any distance—even if there are layered obstacles between you and your dog. This consistency in your communication makes it easier for your dog to understand your wishes in an instant, without hesitation or confusion.

How to Begin

Arrange two jumps and a tunnel as shown in **Figure 10-3**. Position a path marker midway between the first jump and the tunnel opening (indicated by the letter P). You will use this exercise setup first to teach your dog the cue for *Out*, and then to emphasize the difference between the cue for *Out* and the cue for continuing straight ahead.

Position your dog squarely in front of the first jump and lead out as shown in Figure 10-3. Cue your dog to jump. When he takes off for the jump, give a clear *Out* command and signal (flat palm of your left hand with arm extended) as you move toward a point between the tunnel and the first jump. Use small controlled steps and be sure to move toward the marker—not the tunnel itself! When your dog's head has turned toward the tunnel, give your *Tunnel* command.

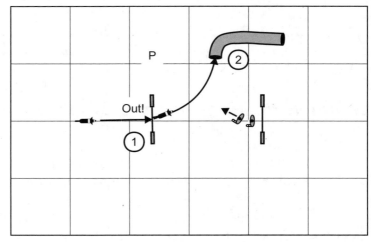

Figure 10-3

If You Have Problems

The two most common problems are dogs that bypass the jump, or bypass the tunnel.

Bypassing the Jump

This can happen if you start moving or turn your shoulders before your dog has taken off for the jump. To avoid this problem, make an effort to remain square with your dog until he has taken off for the jump.

Bypassing the Tunnel

If this happens, freeze and look at your feet. They should be facing the path marker. If you face the tunnel rather than the path, or if you turn your shoulders too soon, you could draw your dog away from the tunnel. With a dog that is slow to turn, keep walking toward your path marker and don't waver from the path until your dog commits to the tunnel. When your dog is first learning this cue, you may need to take several steps toward the marker—perhaps even walk all the way to it. As your dog catches on, fewer and fewer steps will be required. Eventually, all that will be necessary is your verbal command accompanied by a single step with forward pressure toward the path—regardless of how far away you are from your dog.

For the most difficult cases, it may help to show your dog a food-loaded target or toy placed after the tunnel. On the next try, your dog will most likely turn correctly to the tunnel, regardless of your handling. Don't use this as an excuse to handle poorly. Now that the dog is patterned for the behavior you want, your job is to handle correctly, so that you couple the correct behavior with the cue you will use to get that behavior on the agility course.

How to Progress

Once you are successful using *Out* from a position directly ahead of the dog, increase the difficulty by gradually moving your starting position to the side, as shown in **Figure 10-4**. Then, gradually increase your distance as shown in **Figure 10-5.** Follow with other positions and distances ahead of your dog, such as those shown in **Figure 10-6.**

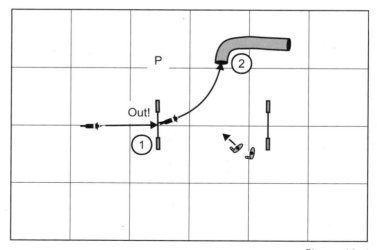

Figure 10-4

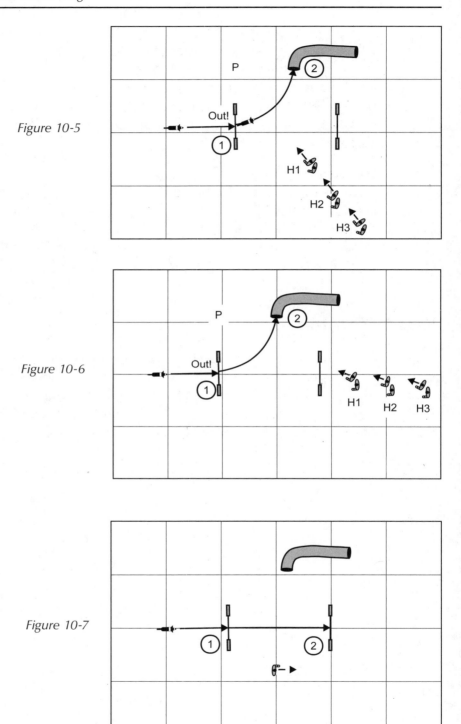

Figure 10-5

Figure 10-6

Figure 10-7

Out vs. Straight Ahead

Before progressing too much further, it's time to emphasize to your dog the difference between your cue to continue ahead versus your cue to turn away from you.

Set your dog up and direct him over the two jumps, as shown in **Figure 10-7**. Since the dog is catching up to your back, your body should be facing parallel to the path you want him to take. This is a markedly different body cue from the one you will use to turn him away from you.

When your dog takes off for the first jump, give your *Jump* command for the second jump. Do not preface it with a *Come* command, even if you are worried that your dog might take the tunnel because he is patterned to do so. You are attempting to teach your dog the cues for each of the two options—straight ahead versus outward turn. You would rarely use a *Come* command between two jumps in a straight-line sequence, so it would be counterproductive and confusing if you used it here.

Since your dog is now patterned to take the tunnel (having recently completed the exercises in Figures 10-4 through 10-6), he may ignore your cue to jump and instead dive into the tunnel. If this happens, block the tunnel opening on the next attempt. Alternatively, you could hold a toy in your signaling hand and throw it over the second jump as you give your command. Give a jackpot reward for success. Once you get a successful two-jump sequence, ask for an *Out* on the next try.

Decreasing Your Lead-Out

As you progress in your *Out* training, gradually reduce your lead-out as shown in **Figure 10-8**. When working from behind the dog, give your *Out* command coupled with a sharp shoulder turn, pressing toward the path marker with the hand closest to your dog—not toward the tunnel.

Randomly alternate between doing the two jumps and doing the *Jump-Out-Tunnel* sequence. When you get the right behavior each time, you'll know you have taught your dog what you intended.

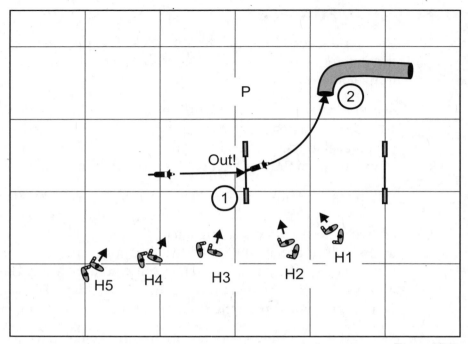

P

Out!

H5   H4   H3   H2   H1

Figure 10-8

Chapter Eleven

Again at a Distance

*A*gain is a command that means "take the obstacle you just performed in the opposite direction." Although not very applicable
to Standard and Jumpers courses, the *Again* command is extremely
useful for accumulating points quickly in Gamblers competition. A dog
that has mastered the *Again* command can whip around and perform
back-to-back tunnels, contacts, weave poles or other bidirectional obstacles with the tightest turns possible and with no wasted time. In the
game of Snooker, the *Again* command is useful for fast back-to-back
performances when your last opening-sequence obstacle and your first
closing-sequence obstacle are the same. In both of these situations, the
ability to use *Again* at a distance is a great asset.

Imagine sending your dog to a tunnel from across the ring and cueing
an *Again* while you position yourself ahead in your planned strategy to
take best advantage of your dog's speed. Having to "be there" to closely
indicate the correct tunnel opening is a disadvantage that limits your
handling options and your ability to get the most points from your run.

An even more valuable use for the *Again* command is for "variations-on-
a-theme" work in your agility training. Once you have patterned your dog
to perform a sequence, you can surprise him with changes of direction
and a random *Again* to keep him on his toes and listening to you. In doing so, you are teaching your dog to listen closely and pay attention to
your commands and signals—not to operate on autopilot. These exercises are unpredictable and fun for you and your dog and keep training
interesting for both of you.

Several of the exercise sets in upcoming chapters of this book will incorporate the *Again* command, so now is a good time to add this skill
to your agility toolbox.

Ideally, it will be to your advantage to teach your dog to *Again* on all of the obstacles that are bidirectional. The best obstacle to use to begin teaching this command is an open tunnel.

Again With the Tunnel

Arrange the tunnel in an arc and position your dog and yourself as shown in **Figure 11-1**. Direct your dog to the tunnel by giving your tunnel command while facing toward the path with a fully extended left signaling arm (the arm closest to your dog). The path is between your dog's current position and the tunnel opening, as indicated by path marker P1. As he exits, command *Again* and step forward toward the new path (P2) with your right foot, signaling a return through the tunnel with your extended right arm. (If necessary, repeat the *Tunnel* command. Eliminate the command for the tunnel, however, as soon as possible. Your dog may be confused about whether you want him to take the tunnel in the opposite direction or whether you want him to take the first end of the tunnel he sees.)

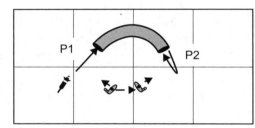

Figure 11-1

To eliminate any ambiguity, be careful to use the proper body position, and face the path you want the dog to take as in Figure 11-1. Over-rotating and facing toward the tunnel opening can cause ambiguity about which side of the tunnel you want the dog to enter, as shown in **Figure 11-2**.

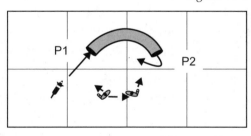

Figure 11-2

A good way to reward your dog for this exercise is by throwing a ball, toy, or food container as your dog completes the second tunnel performance and releasing him with a command to *Get It*. This encourages speed and enthusiasm and helps promote a tight about-turn. Keep in mind, however, that the dog must exit the tunnel with all four feet before re-entering to get credit for completing it.

Occasionally a dog may decide to come toward you rather than repeating the tunnel, despite proper handing on your part. If this happens, position one or two wire guides as a barrier near the tunnel exit as illustrated in **Figure 11-3**. When your dog catches on, you can then eliminate the guides.

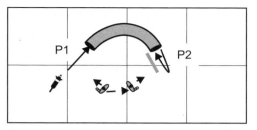

Figure 11-3

Build on success by gradually increasing your distance from your dog, as shown in **Figure 11-4**. Start at position H1 and gradually increase your distance, using starting positions H2 through H4.

Next, gradually eliminate your signal and body movements until your dog can perform an *Again* on a verbal command alone. Although you may (and should) use a signal as well as a verbal command when competing, teach-

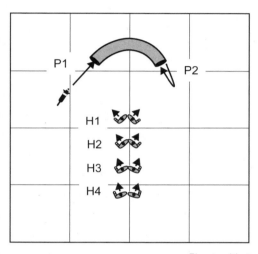

Figure 11-4

ing your dog to respond to the verbal command alone gives you extra insurance that is valuable when your dog is working at a great distance. Moreover, it can often be an advantage to give a jet-propelled dog an *Again* command before he exits the tunnel (before he sees your signal and body position) so he will be prepared to about-turn quickly after he exits. As you did before, gradually increase your distance from your dog, using only a verbal command.

Once you are convinced that your dog understands what you want when you give your *Again* command, it is time to randomly alternate between asking for an *Again* versus asking your dog to *Come* after the first tunnel performance. This will prevent anticipation and teach your dog to pay close attention to your cues when completing an obstacle.

Again With Jumps and the Tire Jump

At this point your dog may think that *Again* means "take the tunnel in the opposite direction." Your dog now needs to apply the concept of *Again* to other obstacles. Your next logical choice is to train *Again* on jumps and the tire. The methods you use are the same for both obstacles.

It will be easiest for your dog to be successful if you begin with the jumps set low. Once your dog catches on to the concept, you can gradually raise the jumps. Additionally, winged jumps are easier than wingless jumps to start with because it is less likely that your dog will choose to run around them.

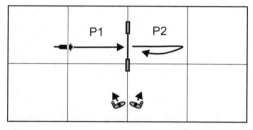

Figure 11-5

Position your dog and yourself as shown in **Figure 11-5**. Direct your dog to complete the jump and immediately command and signal an *Again* as you did for the tunnel. As before, be sure to face the dog's path rather than the obstacle and use the signaling arm closest to the dog for each command to jump. If your dog tries to return to you rather than take the jump after the *Again* command, use wire guides or other barriers to help your dog be successful as shown in **Figure 11-6**. Gradually increase your distance from the jump as shown in **Figure 11-7**. Then, work through the same progression using only verbal commands.

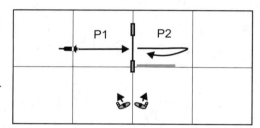

Figure 11-6

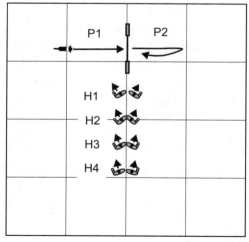

Figure 11-7

Again With the Contact Obstacles

You are ready to train *Again* with contact obstacles only after your contact performance is fast and accurate without the use of targets and at a variety of distances. Since the seesaw is not bi-directional, the dogwalk and A-frame are the only contacts you will train with the *Again* command. The procedures for the dogwalk and A-frame are identical, so you can begin with either obstacle.

> *Here's a bit of historical agility trivia: In the early days of USDAA competition, it was legal to perform an* **Again** *on the seesaw in the Gamblers class. It was a great way to accumulate points in a hurry, so several of us (at least in our area of the country) trained our dogs to exit the seesaw, whip around and place a paw on the downside to prevent it from resetting, then race to complete the seesaw in the opposite direction. It was quite fun! It is no longer legal, however, so you should limit your* **Again** *training to the A-frame and dogwalk.*

Position your dog and yourself as shown in **Figure 11-8**. Direct your dog to complete the dogwalk. As he reaches the desired downside contact position, command and signal an *Again* as you did for the tunnels and jumps. (Make sure all four of your dog's feet exit the plank before ascending for the second time.)

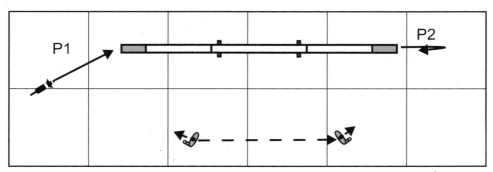

Figure 11-8

As before, be sure to face the path rather than the obstacle and use the signaling arm closest to the dog. If your dog tries to return to you rather than take the dogwalk after the *Again* command, use wire guides or other barriers (shown in **Figure 11-9**) to help your dog be successful.

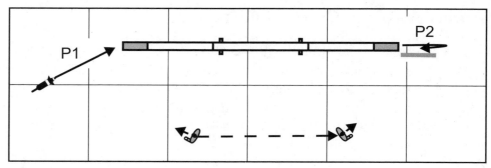

Figure 11-9

Gradually increase your distance from the dogwalk as shown in **Figure 11-10**. Then, work through the same progression using only verbal commands.

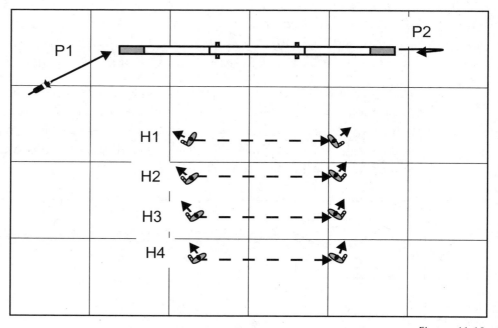

Figure 11-10

Again with the Weave Poles

Do not attempt to train *Again* with the weave poles until your obstacle performance is fast and accurate at a variety of distances.

Position your dog and yourself as shown in **Figure 11-11**. Direct your dog to complete the weave poles and immediately command and signal an *Again* as you did for the other obstacles. Be sure to face the dog's path rather than the obstacle and use the signaling arm closest to the dog.

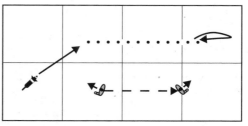

Figure 11-11

If your dog tries to return to you rather than re-enter the weave poles after the *Again* command, use wire guides or other barriers, as shown in **Figure 11-12**, to help your dog be successful.

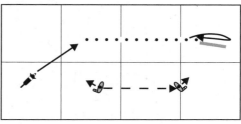

Figure 11-12

Gradually increase your distance from the weave poles as shown in **Figure 11-13**. Then, work through the same progression using only verbal commands.

Once successful with the *Again* command, don't forget to randomly alternate between *Again* and *Come* after the first performance of the obstacle.

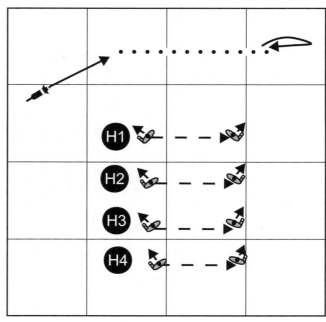

Figure 11-13

RANDALL KNAPP

Chapter Twelve

Contact/Tunnel Flips at a Distance

A familiar element in many agility courses is an outward 180-degree flip from a contact obstacle to an adjacent tunnel. It is a great advantage to have trained your dog to perform this maneuver with tight efficiency—without wasting any yardage or time. In **Figure 12-1** you can see an efficient flip turn into the tunnel. Contrast this with the inefficient flip shown in **Figure 12-2**. It is an even greater advantage to be able to direct your dog through this maneuver from a variety of distances—especially from behind or from a wide lateral handling position.

To train your dog to respond to your cue for the contact/tunnel flip at a distance, you must have a dog that performs the contact obstacles with speed and accuracy, regardless of your handling position. If this skill is lacking, revisit **Chapter 4: Contact Obstacles at a Distance,** before attempting this exercise. You will also need to have trained the *Out* command, covered in **Chapter 10: Lateral Pushing Using the Out Command.**

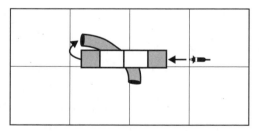

Figure 12-1

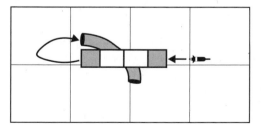

Figure 12-2

Consider a course segment with a three-jump straightaway followed by the dogwalk and an outward flip to the tunnel, as shown in **Figure 12-3**. In this example, the ability to direct your dog from the dogwalk to the tunnel from a distance behind your dog allows you to position yourself optimally for the upcoming sequence. When your dog exits the tunnel it is easy to pull him to #5 and continue through #8. Your handing position makes it easy for him to read the course and complete it as smoothly and efficiently as possible.

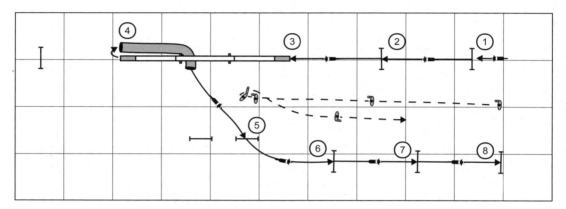

Figure 12-3

This "flip-at-a-distance" skill also allows you to take full advantage of your dog's speed with no wasted time. Consider what would happen if you needed to be alongside your dog at the end of the dogwalk to direct him to the tunnel. (Assume the sequence is in the middle of a course and you could not get ahead of your dog at jump #1.) In this situation, it is likely that your dog would reach the end of the dogwalk before you do. This is especially likely if you have followed the procedures in **Chapter 4** and have trained your dog to perform all of the obstacles at your dog's fastest speed, regardless of your body position. If your dog reaches the end of the dogwalk ahead of you, one of two things might happen. If your dog has a solid two-on/two-off contact performance, your well-trained dog will wait in position while you catch up—as precious seconds tick away. If he is not solid on his position or if you have trained a running contact, it is likely he will exit the dogwalk before you have reached the end. Because you are running full-tilt to catch up with him, your body language tells him to take the jump directly ahead, resulting in a wrong-course fault as shown in **Figure 12-4.**

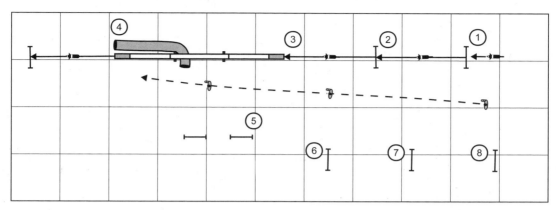

Figure 12-4

If you could keep up with your dog, or if he firmly held his contact while you raced to catch up, you might be faced with a possible off-course or a crunchy handler collision after the tunnel because micromanaging the flip puts you in a poor position to indicate jump #5 as you can see in **Figure 12-5**.

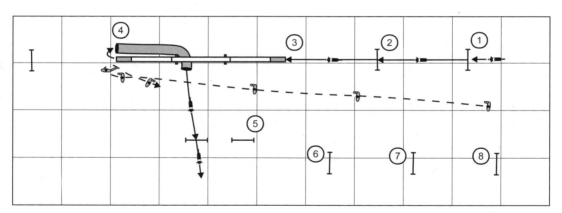

Figure 12-5

Figure 12-6 shows another example of a course segment in which the ability to direct an outward flip from a wide lateral distance is an advantage. By staying wide, the handler is able to smoothly indicate the transition from #5 to #6. If you needed to be near your dog to indicate the tunnel, there is a good chance you would not be able to be in a good position to indicate #6 by the time your dog exited the tunnel. This could lead to an off-course fault as shown in **Figure 12-7**. Alternatively, it could lead to a handler collision, a knocked bar, or run-out at jump #6.

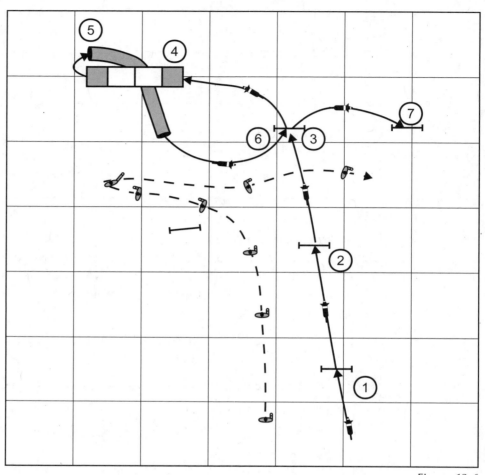

Figure 12-6

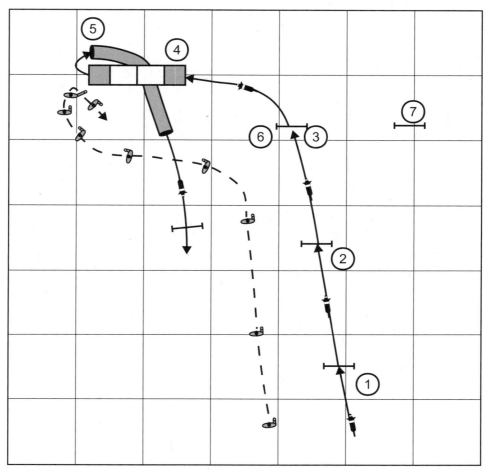

Figure 12-7

The Flip From in Front

Set up a dogwalk and tunnel as shown in **Figure 12-8**. (It's best to start with a dogwalk rather than an A-frame because it is less steep, which will make it easier for your dog.) It may be helpful to initially position wire guides or other barriers, as shown, to help your dog be successful.

Begin by teaching the cue for a flip. To isolate this behavior, start by picking up your dog and placing him in the two-on/two-off position. If you have a very large dog or a dog that resents being picked up, you can instead ask your dog to perform the entire dogwalk with each repetition. If you do this, however, you must be certain that your dog's speed and accuracy are maintained on each and every attempt.

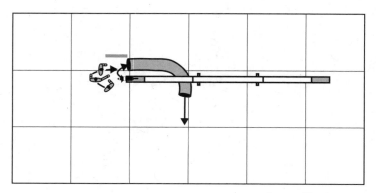

Figure 12-8

It's easiest for your dog to understand the cue for a tight flip when you are in a clear position in front of him, so this is a good place to start. Position your dog and yourself as shown in Figure 12-8. Fully extend the arm closest to your dog (in this example, your right arm) straight ahead of you. Give your *Out* command (which is a turn away from the handler). Use your right arm and hand to smoothly trace the path you want your dog to take, that is, a tight arc from the dogwalk to the tunnel. At the same time, walk in a tight U-shaped path as you lead through the turn with your left shoulder. Smoothly transfer your signal from your right arm to your left as you complete your turn. When your dog sees the tunnel, give him your *Tunnel* command and reward generously as he exits with a thrown toy or food container and a release to *Get It*.

If You Have Problems

Your dog may have **gone back up the dogwalk**. This can happen if you begin your signal for the flip with the hand farthest from your dog. When you do so, your signal could be easily misinterpreted as a cue for *Again* (covered in **Chapter 11**) meaning "take the last obstacle you took in the opposite direction." Try again, this time making sure to start the turn with the hand closest to your dog, and walking a U-shaped path. Don't transfer your signal to your left hand until your dog has turned and is looking at the tunnel.

Your dog may have **stayed on the contact or hesitated at the tunnel opening**. To avoid this problem, on the next attempt, keep your feet moving, lead with your shoulder, and don't wait for your dog to move. Start moving and expect him to follow your lead. If your dog still doesn't respond, take him by the collar or tab and gently launch him toward the tunnel. Follow with enthusiastic praise and reward as he exits. Alternatively, you could show him a baited target placed after the exit of the tunnel to help him be more successful on the next try.

You may have **gotten a spin between the dogwalk and tunnel**. On your next attempt, make sure you are not first pulling the dog toward you and then pushing him toward the tunnel. Instead, signal an outward turn immediately from the dogwalk. Reward only performances made without a spin.

The Flip From the Side

Once your dog has mastered the flip from in front, train him to respond to your cue from the side. It may be helpful to position an additional barrier as shown in **Figure 12-9** to help ensure initial success. Your goal is to remain behind the dotted handler line for the entire sequence. If you cross the handler line, you could easily pull your dog away from the tunnel as you pull out to get around the dogwalk. Start wide enough from the dogwalk so that you can take a U-shaped path without crossing the handler line.

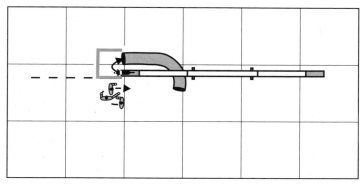

Figure 12-9

Gradually add lateral distance and remove the barriers as your dog catches on as shown in **Figures 12-10 through 12-12**.

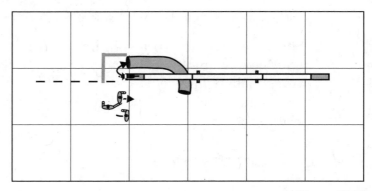

Figure 12-10

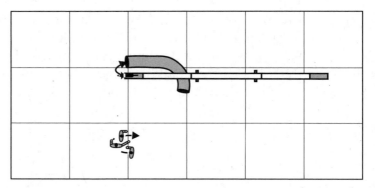

Figure 12-11

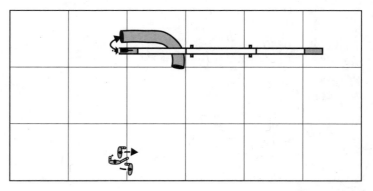

Figure 12-12

At this point your dog has become quite familiar with the cue for the outward flip. Before going any further it's time to emphasize the difference between the cue to turn away from you and the cue to turn toward you. This step is important to ensure that your dog is listening and paying attention to your cues, not merely operating on autopilot. On your next attempt, instead of asking for a flip, ask for a different sequence, as shown in **Figure 12-13**.

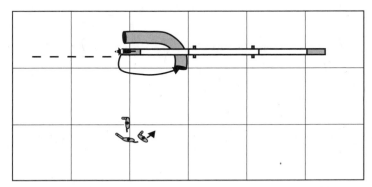

Figure 12-13

Next, make sure your flip command works when you have a layered obstacle between you and your dog as shown in **Figure 12-14**.

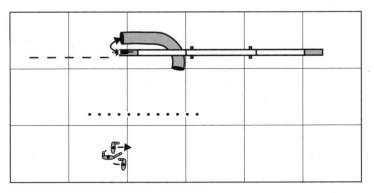

Figure 12-14

The Flip From Behind

Once your dog has mastered the flip from a lateral distance, it is time to start working on cueing the flip from behind. To make it easy for your dog to be successful, begin this training from a wide lateral distance as shown in **Figure 12-15**. This way, your dog can see you most easily in his peripheral vision.

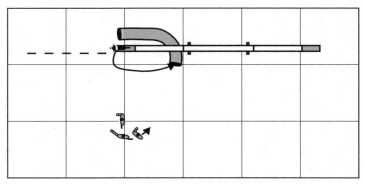

Figure 12-15

Gradually increase your distance behind him while staying wide as shown in **Figure 12-16**.

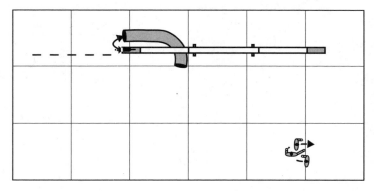

Figure 12-16

Next, position yourself closer to the dogwalk as shown in **Figure 12-17** and gradually increase your distance behind him as in **Figure 12-18**. Eventually, vary the sequence on occasion as in Figure 12-13 to keep him on his toes and listening to you.

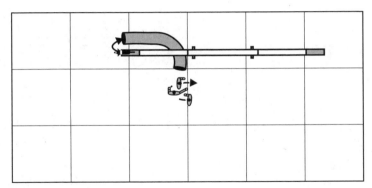

Figure 12-17

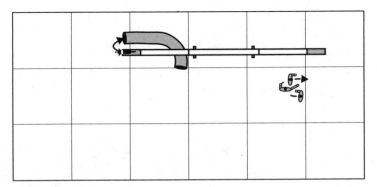

Figure 12-18

How to Progress

Next, work though all of the exercises in Figures 12-8 through 12-18, adding the actual performance of the dogwalk before your cue for a flip, rather than placing him on the downside contact to begin.

Then, repeat the entire progression with an A-frame-to-tunnel sequence.

RANDALL KNAPP

Chapter Thirteen

More Fun With Concentric Circles

In *Chapter 9: Lateral Distance Through Circle Training,* you discovered the fun and training value of directing your dog through circles of obstacles from a center position. In subsequent chapters you have mastered new skills such as *Out, Again,* and outward 180-degree flips. Armed with all of these valuable skills, you are now ready to try a more advanced and enormously fun set of exercises, all of which capitalize on working through variations on a theme to sharpen your dog's responses. Through patterning sequences and then injecting unexpected variations, your dog learns to pay close attention to your commands and body cues, rather than operating on autopilot. The sequences are unpredictable for your dog, which makes your training sessions fun for both of you.

To start, arrange two concentric circles of jumps and tunnels, such as the setup shown in **Figure 13-1**. Handling from an area in the center, direct your dog to perform the inner circle of obstacles as in **Figure 13-2**. If successful, direct him to perform the outer circle as shown in **Figure 13-3**. These tasks should be a breeze since you have mastered them through the exercises in *Chapter 9: Lateral Distance Through Circle Training.* If these sequences are not fast and flawless, go back and rework them before continuing.

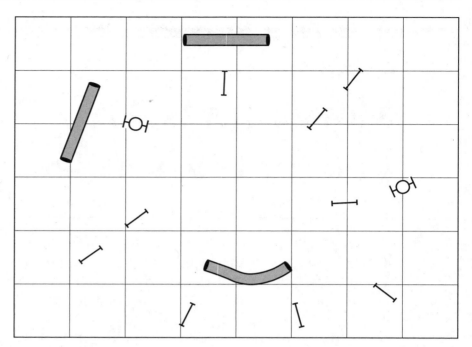

Figure 13-1

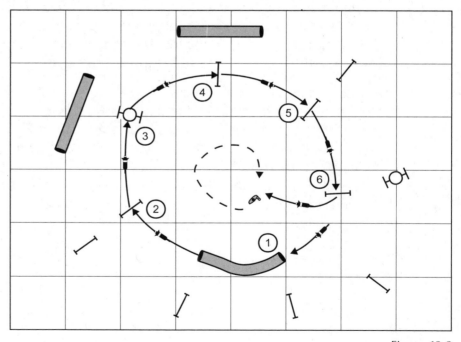

Figure 13-2

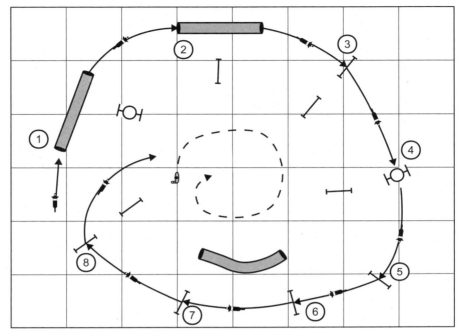

Figure 13-3

Inner/Outer Loop Sequences

Once you have mastered both inner and outer circles, the real fun begins. Using the same setup, start your dog on the inner circle as shown in **Figure 13-4**. For this and for all of the remaining illustrations in this chapter, the handler and dog start positions are indicated by the letter S. Begin with the #1 tunnel. As soon as your dog commits to the following jump, use your *Out* command and signal to push him to the outer circle. (Face path marker P1 and signal with your fully outstretched left signaling arm, which is the arm closest to your dog). Follow with the command for the tunnel the moment he sees it.

Continue with the second tunnel, while facing path marker P2. Immediately before your dog exits, give your *Come* command. As he exits the tunnel, bring your signaling arm in close to your body and face parallel to the path you want your dog to take. When he sees the correct jump on the inner circle, give your *Jump* command. As he takes off for the jump use your *Out* command and signal to push him to the outer circle. (Face path marker P3 and signal with your fully outstretched left signaling arm.) Follow with the command for the tire the moment he sees it. Finish by calling your dog to you after the tire.

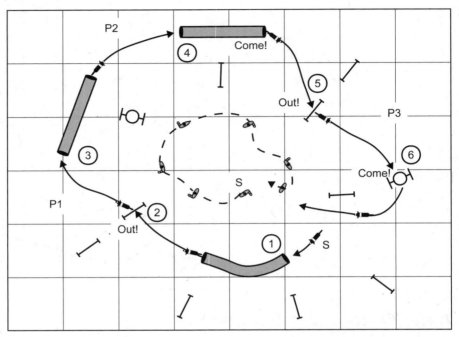

Figure 13-4

Other examples of inner/outer loop sequences using the same setup are shown in **Figures 13-5 and 13-6**. Use your imagination to come up with other variations. The possibilities are endless!

Throughout your sequencing, keep in mind the following:

◆ If the next obstacle is in line with your dog's current path and no directional change is required, give your command for the next obstacle.

◆ If your dog needs to turn outward laterally away from you, give your *Out* command and signal.

◆ If your dog needs to turn toward you to see the next obstacle, turn parallel to the path you want him to take and give your *Come* command. When he sees the correct obstacle, give your obstacle command.

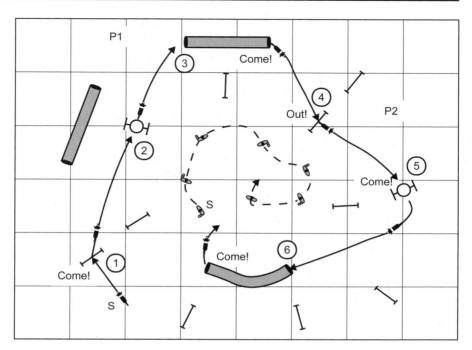

Figure 13-5

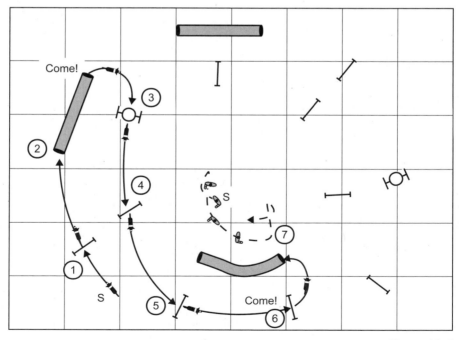

Figure 13-6

Regarding your signals, also keep in mind the following:

♦ To push your dog out or to keep him out, use a fully outstretched signaling arm and face the path (between your dog's current position and the next obstacle you want him to take).

♦ To bring your dog in, bring your signaling arm in close to you and turn your entire body parallel to the path you want your dog to take.

♦ As with every exercise, if your dog makes a mistake, stop right away. Then, isolate and work through the problem before continuing.

Using the Again Command

Using the *Again* command (which means "take the last obstacle you took in the opposite direction"), you can inject immediate changes in direction within either of the circles. An example is shown in **Figure 13-7**.

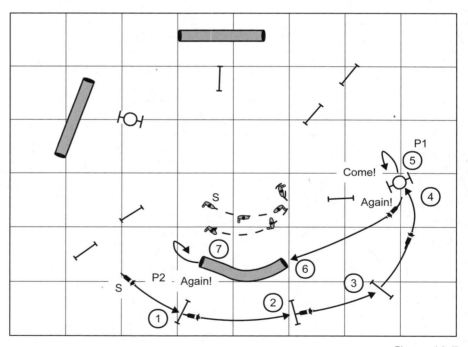

Figure 13-7

Get your dog started with the three-jump sequence on the outer loop. As your dog takes off for the #4 tire, give your *Again* command and signal. Because you are now working the dog off your left, use your left hand and outstretched signaling arm to push toward path marker P1. A command for the tire is not needed since this is indicated by the *Again* command. Call your dog to the tunnel on the inner circle and follow with an immediate *Again* command, as you face P2. Keep in mind that your dog must exit the tunnel with all four feet before going back in the opposite direction!

Incorporating 180-Degree Outward Flips

Any time that you are sequencing through the inner circle, you can use your *Out* command and body cue for a flip to push your dog into the outer circle, traveling in the opposite direction as shown in **Figure 13-8**.

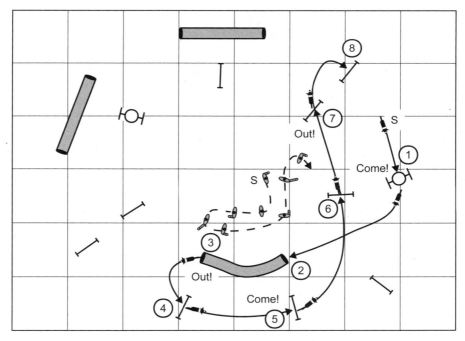

Figure 13-8

Begin with the tire and pull to the tunnel. Before your dog exits, give your *Out* command. As he exits, flip your left signaling arm outward (tracing the path you want your dog to take) and immediately walk in a tight, counterclockwise U-shaped path. As you do so, smoothly transfer the signal from your left to your right hand. Give your command for the jump as soon as he sees it. Continue through the next two jumps. When he commits to the third, give your *Out* command, flip your right signaling arm outward while making a clockwise U-turn, and smoothly transfer your signal from your right to your left hand. Give your *Jump* command the moment he sees the correct one.

Combining Maneuvers

Next, use your imagination to devise variations that combine all of the maneuvers you have practiced thus far. An example is shown in **Figure 13-9**.

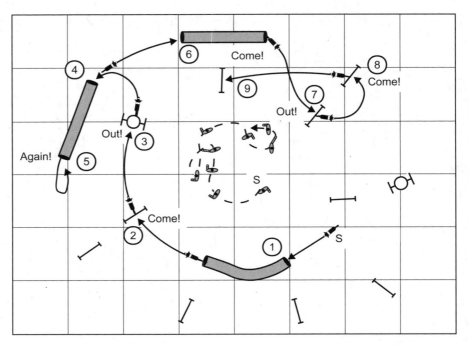

Figure 13-9

Adding Obstacles

Once your dog is doing well using simple obstacles such as tunnels and jumps, add more complex ones such as contact obstacles, weave poles, and the pause table (**Figure 13-10**). Remember: you must already have trained speed and accuracy at a distance on each of these obstacles. If these skills are lacking, go back and master them before continuing. Follow the same training progression of first patterning your dog to perform each circle of obstacles.

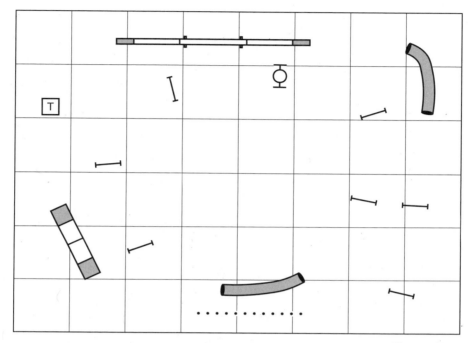

Figure 13-10

Next you can progress to inner/outer loop sequences. Some examples are shown in **Figures 13-11 and 13-12**. To ensure straight approaches and exits both to and from contact obstacles, you may find it helpful to position wire guides at the plank entrances and exits. Likewise, you may want to use guides to ensure correct weave-pole entries and exits. Once your dog has mastered the exercises using the guides, you can gradually remove them.

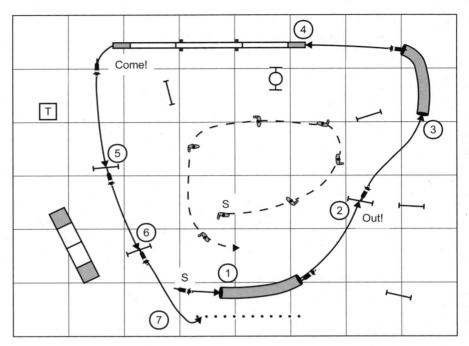

Figure 13-11

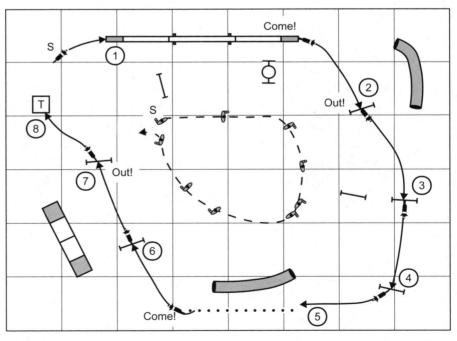

Figure 13-12

An example of a sequence using the *Again* command on a contact obstacle is shown in **Figure 13-13**. Bear in mind that your dog must exit the contact planks with all four feet before remounting the plank.

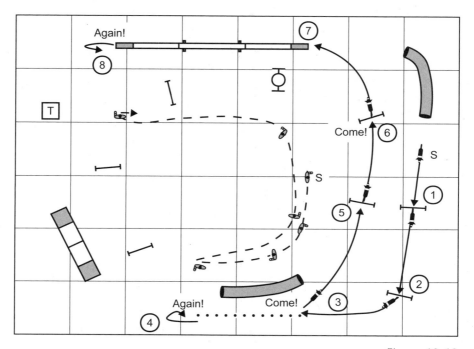

Figure 13-13

Examples of sequences incorporating 180-degree inward and outward flips are shown in **Figures 13-14 and 13-15**, respectively. Finally, devise variations that combine several maneuvers, as shown by the example in **Figure 13-16**.

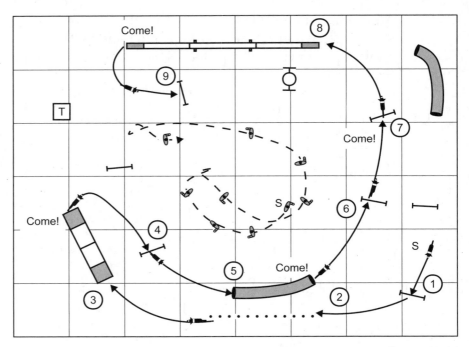

Figure 13-14

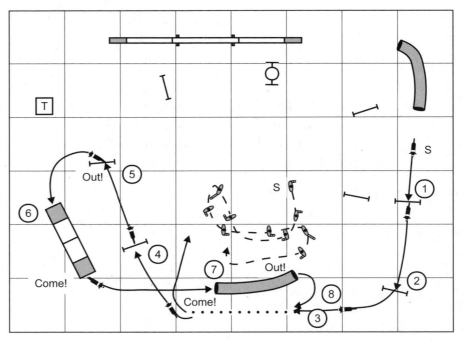

Figure 13-15

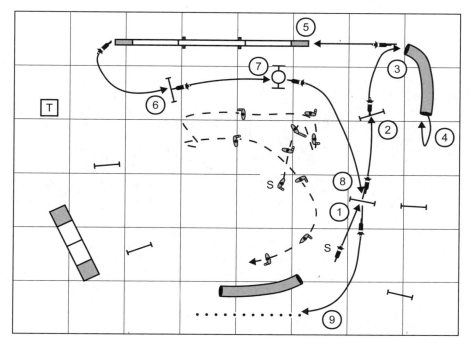

Figure 13-16

The more comfortable you become with these valuable distance skills—when they are business-as-usual for you and your dog—the more you will enjoy choosing and using them in competition. At the same time, you will gain a whole new level of handling flexibility that can truly improve your dog's ring performances.

Chapter Fourteen

Linear-Distance Skills

Dogs vary greatly in their linear-distance threshold—that is, the distance they will confidently work ahead of their handlers. This distance is usually shorter for smaller or slower dogs. When dogs reach their linear-distance threshold, they tend to check back with their handlers or resist venturing ahead any farther. Your goal is to extend your dog's threshold until he is comfortable working at the maximum distance he will encounter in competition, and then some. If your dog will send through a 40-yard sequence in practice, he should have no trouble with a 25-yard sequence under the excitement and distracting conditions of the competition ring.

How to Begin

In early chapters of this book you learned to send your dog to every agility obstacle from a variety of angles and distances. Therefore, you have already completed the first step in your linear-distance training. Now you will learn to send your dog straight ahead of you to perform sequences of two or more obstacles.

One of the best methods to accomplish this goal is by backchaining. You start by having your dog complete the final part of the sequence. Gradually, you add more obstacles to the front part of the sequence until your dog can complete the entire sequence on his own. In this way, your dog is always traveling to a familiar and rewarding end point. This helps your dog be successful and builds confidence in his ability to work away from you.

Start with a sequence of four jumps leading in a straight line to a table as shown in **Figure 14-1**. Space the jumps 15' apart, and place a visible, food-loaded target on the back of the table. Your goal is to train your dog to send over all four jumps to the table, while you remain behind the farthest jump.

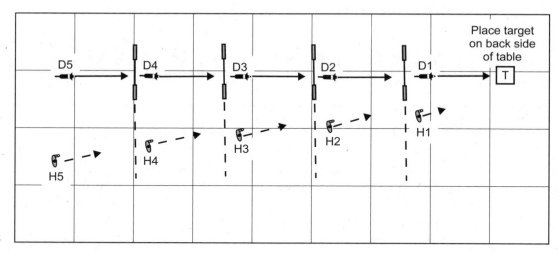

Figure 14-1

Start by showing your dog a treat on a target placed at the back of the table, but don't let him eat it. With you and your dog in positions H1 and D1, respectively, send your dog to the table. To do so, give your command for the table while signaling with the hand closest to your dog. You may take several small steps forward as shown in Figure 14-1, however, try to come to a gliding halt at least 8′ from the table.

The moment your dog leaves the ground for the table, give him a command to *Get It* which releases him to the target. Do not ask for a sit or down. This is important because if your dog doesn't sit or down immediately, you should not reward him. As such, you will lose the opportunity to reinforce him for running smoothly and quickly to the table, which is the point of the training exercise. Instead, while he is eating his treat, run up to join him at the table, pet and praise him while he is on it, then release.

TRAINING TIP: *Don't be lazy and call your dog off of the table to reward him. This will only encourage him to momentarily touch the table top and then bank off of it to return to you. This is a bad habit that could later haunt you during future pause-table performances. Keep in mind that the* **Table** *command means to "find the table and jump on it." Your dog may remain in any position but he may not jump off until released with a* **Come** *command, an obstacle command, or a release word.*

If successful, progress to starting positions H2 and D2. Give your *Jump* command and start taking small, controlled steps forward, in a slightly converging path. (Be sure to keep your outside shoulder angled slightly inward.) When your dog leaves the ground for the jump, give an enthusiastic command for the table, while coming to a smooth and gliding halt behind the dashed handling line. As your dog leaves the ground for the table, release him to the target with a command to *Get It*.

NOTE: *Give a fully extended arm signal when you want your dog to work away from you. A signal with your elbow bent and hand close to your body can transmit uncertainty on your part. What's more, withdrawing your signal into your body or dropping it abruptly before your dog has committed to an obstacle can make him think you've changed your mind.*

After each new success, start farther back in the jump sequence. As you back up, leave more lateral distance between you and your dog, which will enable you to give the most effective body cues.

As you increase your starting distance from the table, you may find it helpful to begin stacking your commands. Stacking means giving your command for the next obstacle a half-second or so earlier than you would if you were running with your dog. This helps minimize the chance that your dog will decide to turn back to you before completing the exercise.

TRAINING TIP: *Your tone of voice is especially important when you are sending your dog to work by himself. The more confident and enthusiastic you sound, the more successful you will tend to be. Conversely, if you sound unsure or hesitant, your dog will probably be as well.*

When you have progressed to successfully sending your dog through the entire five-obstacle sequence, you can begin to wean him off the target. To do this, show your dog a treat placed on the target, and then remove it when he isn't looking. Send him through the sequence, and when he jumps on the table, run up and reward him by placing a treat on the target.

Eventually, you can switch to a less visible target—one that blends in more with the table top. Start by sending your dog through the sequence to a baited target. Then, sometimes bait it and sometimes run up and reward him yourself. Eventually you will be able to remove the target completely.

If You Have Problems

Your dog may have **stopped and looked back to you for guidance**. This is a very common reaction when beginning your linear-distance training. If this happens, don't repeat your command! If you do, you will be teaching your dog to check back with you and earn refusals. You will also be teaching him that it isn't important to respond to your first command. Instead, break the exercise off and try again, making it easier on your next attempt.

You could have caused the problem through **late commands**. If possible, work with a friend to improve your command timing.

The problem could also be caused by **poor body language**. If you start too close to your dog, you could end up pulling away from him as you move ahead, which could draw him out of the line of obstacles. From your dog's point of view, starting wider (at a greater lateral distance) from him and moving gradually inward makes your wishes much clearer.

How to Progress

To make the exercise more challenging, gradually increase the spacing between the jumps until they are spaced 25′ apart.

Eventually, you can inject variations to keep your dog on his toes and listening to you. You do not want him to always assume the next obstacle he sees in his path is correct. Surprise him with random call-offs as illustrated in **Figure 14-2**.

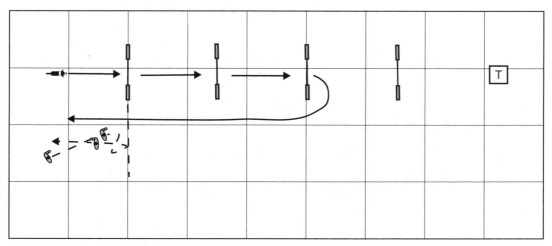

Figure 14-2

After successfully calling your dog off, follow immediately by sending him through the entire sequence, as shown in **Figure 14-3**. Doing so will reinforce your dog's understanding of the distinct cues you will use for different sequence options.

Using the same procedure, you can eventually create other linear-distance exercises using a variety of more challenging obstacles. Some examples are shown in **Figures 14-4 through 14-7**. For each exercise, begin by backchaining the last two obstacles while you remain behind the first obstacle. Then, add to the length of the sequence one obstacle at a time, only when the previous sequence is fast and flawless. As you add obstacles, remember to start from a progressively wider lateral position, so that you will be able to converge as your dog performs the sequence.

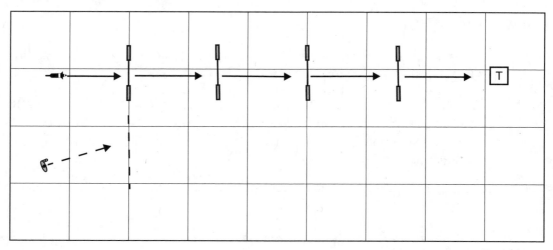

Figure 14-3

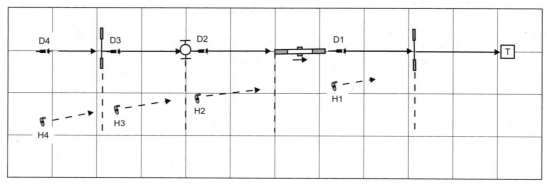

Figure 14-4

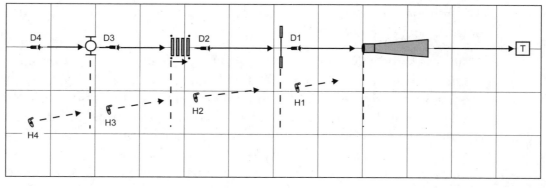

Figure 14-5

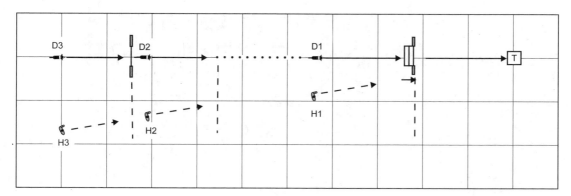

Figure 14-6

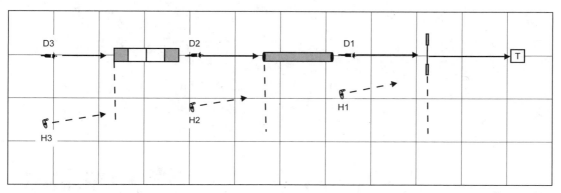

Figure 14-7

Chapter Fifteen

Combining Flips and Layering

I n *Chapter 12: Contact/Tunnel Flips at a Distance,* you were introduced to 180-degree flips from a contact obstacle to an adjacent tunnel. In this chapter, you will use the same cue to perform flips from a tunnel to a jump. This fun exercise allows you to work on both flips and layering skills. At the same time, it encourages you to train "variations on a theme," which will keep your dog thinking and responding to your cues.

How to Begin

Arrange four jumps and a tunnel as shown in **Figure 15-1**. To make it easy for your dog to be success-ful, position jumps #2 through #4 in contact with the tunnel, so it is impossible for your dog to run between them. It's best to begin with the jumps set low. You can raise them later when the exercises are mastered.

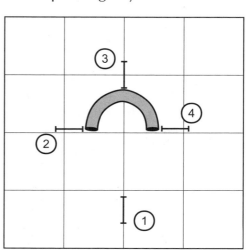

Figure 15-1

Step #1: Perform the Outside Loop

First, direct your dog around the outside loop of jumps, as shown in **Figure 15-2**. Try not to cross the dashed handling line that extends from the inside edge of the tunnel. By staying behind it, you can keep your movements smooth throughout the sequence. Crossing the dashed line could cause you to get trapped behind the tunnel, which could impede your movements and may cause your dog to hesitate or pull off one of the jumps.

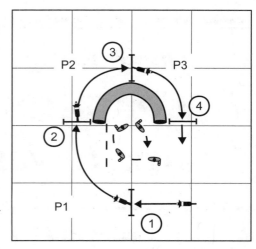

Figure 15-2

Remember to continuously face the path for the outside loop. This means when your dog is in midair over #1, you should be facing path marker P1; when he's in midair over jump #2, you should be facing P2; and when he's in midair over #3, you should be facing P3. The entire time, however, you should keep moving with small, fluid steps. If successful, perform the mirror image of this exercise with your dog working on your right.

If You Have Problems

If your dog **sucks into the tunnel,** block it with a wire guide or other barrier. Once successful, remove the barrier and try again.

If your dog is **confused about how to negotiate the jump sequence** with you on the opposite side of the tunnel, a good training aid to use is a toy-on-a-stick as seen in **Figure 15-3**. Hold the stick in your signaling hand (the hand closest to your dog) and lure your dog through the jump sequence. Let him attack the toy after he clears the last jump. For dogs that prefer food, you can hang a toy stuffed with food at the end of the stick. Once your dog has caught on to the sequence, you can eliminate the stick. Another benefit of the toy-on-a-stick is that using it will help you face the correct direction while keeping your movements smooth and flowing.

Step #2: Perform the Inside Loop

Now that your dog is patterned to take the outside loop, it's time to take the inside loop as shown in **Figure 15-4**. As your dog commits to jump #1, give your command to *Come* as you turn sharply, bring your signaling arm in close to your body, and face parallel to the path you want your dog to take. Give your *Tunnel* command when he has turned and

Figure 15-3

sees the tunnel. Give huge rewards for following your cues. If successful, perform the mirror image of this exercise with the dog on your right.

If You Have Problems

If your dog **insists on taking an outside jump rather than the tunnel,** despite good command timing and correct body cues, have a friend stand in front of the jump on the next try, blocking the incorrect choice. Follow with a huge reward for success. Gradually eliminate the help.

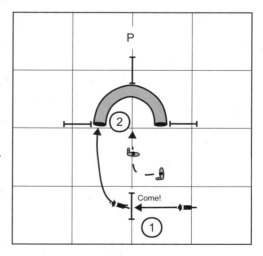

Figure 15-4

Step #3: Move the Jumps Farther Out

When you can alternate randomly between the exercises in Steps 1 and 2—and always get the correct choice—you are ready to make the exercise more challenging. Move the jumps just far enough from the walls of the tunnel so that it is possible for your dog to run between them.

Direct your dog through the sequence as shown in **Figure 15-5**. Again, be sure to keep your path outside of a line made by the inside edge of the tunnel. If you do cross the line, it is likely that your dog will miss jump #3, as illustrated in **Figure 15-6**.

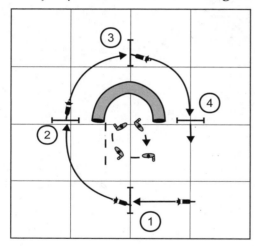 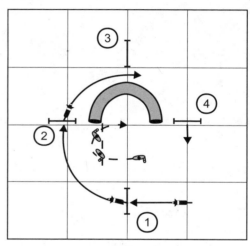

Figure 15-5   Figure 15-6

Step #4: Add the Flip

Next, ask for the tunnel as shown in **Figure 15-7**. As he enters the tunnel, quickly back up to give yourself room for the next maneuver. As your dog exits the tunnel, give your *Out* command (which is a turn away from the handler) and signal a flip to jump #3. Begin the signal using the arm closest to your dog (your left arm), smoothly tracing the path you want your dog to take. At the same time, walk in a tight U-shaped path as you signal your dog through the turn. Follow with your command for jump #3. As he commits to #3, smoothly transfer your signal from your left arm to your right and give your command and signal for jump #4 while facing path marker P.

Finish with jump #5 off your right. If successful, perform the mirror image of the exercise starting with the dog on you right.

If You Have Problems

If your dog **has trouble with the flip**, isolate the maneuver by performing only obstacles #2 and #3. It may help to place a target after #3 or to throw a toy with your signaling hand as you command him to jump. Alternatively, you could use a toy-on-a-stick to guide your dog through the maneuver. Once the #2 to #3 sequence is smooth, you can add the other obstacles back into the exercise.

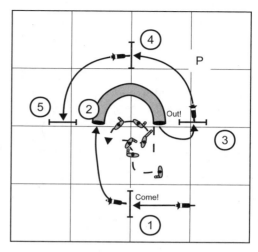

Figure 15-7

If your dog **spins after the flip**, break off the exercise. A spin often occurs when you cue your dog to take a flat approach to the #3 jump as illustrated in **Figure 15-8**. You can help cue your dog for the correct upcoming turn from #3 to #4 by rounding out or "molding" the turn from #2 to #3. Use your signal and body language to give your dog a rounded approach to #3 and following through with your

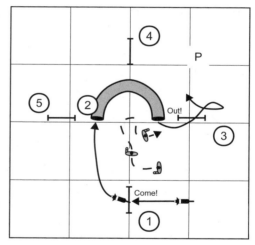

Figure 15-8

signal and body language so that he will know which way he will be turning before he takes off for the jump.

If your dog **misses jump #4**, break off the exercise. This can happen if you cross the dashed handling line. Doing so makes it difficult for you to face the path marker P between jumps #3 and #4. Try again, this time making an effort to remain behind the line and to face P after your dog has committed to jump #3.

Step #5: Increase Spacing

Move the outermost jump out to a distance of 4' from the tunnel and repeat the progression as shown in **Figures 15-9 and 15-10**. Then add another jump and increase the spacing from the tunnel to the two farthest jumps as shown in **Figures 15-11 and 15-12**.

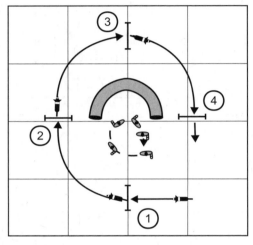

Figure 15-9

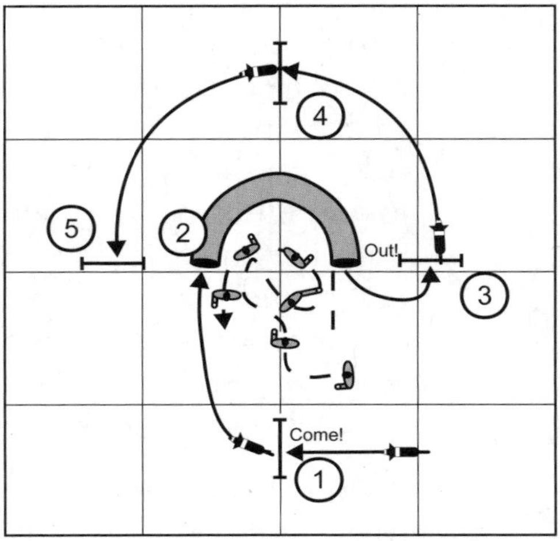

Figure 15-10

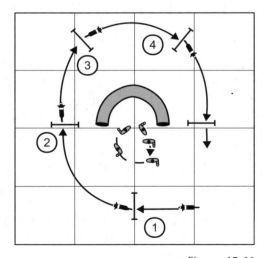

Figure 15-11

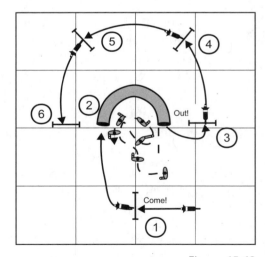

Figure 15-12

Step #6: Add Variations

Use your imagination to create variations using the same setup. Some examples are shown in **Figures 15-13 and 15-14**. Don't forget to try mirror images off the opposite side for all of your variations!

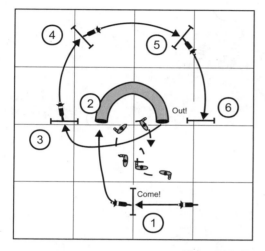

Figure 15-13   *Figure 15-14*

RANDALL KNAPP

Chapter Sixteen
Distance Racetracks

I n this chapter you will experience some fast-paced fun through a set of exercises that combine lateral with linear distance skills. I call them "distance racetracks." An example of a racetrack setup is shown in **Figure 16-1**.

Similar to distance circles, racetracks are great confidence-builders that teach dogs to love working at a distance. For dogs that already thrive on distance work, racetracks provide an excellent means of working on control at high speed. Advanced racetrack exercises that incorporate sequence variations teach your dog to pay close attention to your cues.

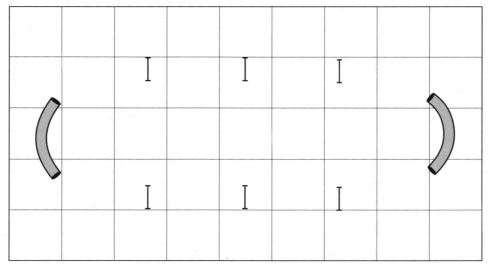

Figure 16-1

Racetracks From the Center

Start by handling from a central position, as shown in **Figure 16-2**. The dashed rectangle defines your handling area. You must remain inside the handling box for all of the following exercise variations.

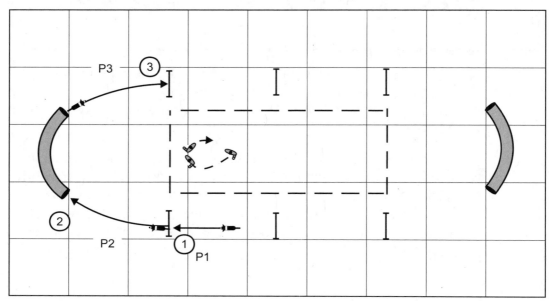

Figure 16-2

Using an offset start as shown, direct your dog through the three-obstacle sequence at one end of the racetrack. This sequence is quite similar to an exercise you mastered in *Chapter 7: Sequencing Using Lateral Distance.* To review, keep in mind the following: When your dog is in his starting position, lead out laterally as shown and face "the path" (represented by path marker P1), which is halfway between the dog's current position and the next obstacle you want him to take. When he is in midair over the first jump, you should be facing P2. When he exits the tunnel you should be facing P3. Use a smooth, continuous signal with the hand and fully extended arm closest to your dog, and keep your feet moving in small, fluid steps. Stopping abruptly or keeping your feet planted while moving only your upper body can give an ambiguous message to your dog. If you have problems with this sequence, revisit the exercises in *Chapter 7* before continuing.

Once you are successful, add a jump to the beginning and to the end of the sequence, as shown in **Figure 16-3.** Again, begin with a lateral lead-out and take a slightly converging path down the line of jumps.

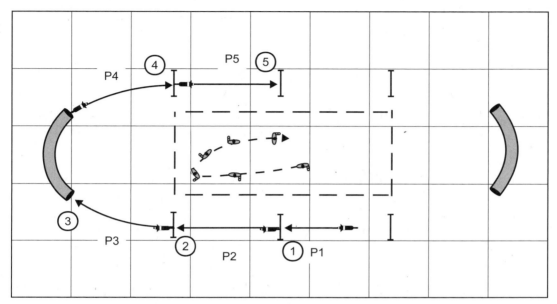

Figure 16-3

Next, direct your dog through the entire racetrack from the center handling box as seen in **Figure 16-4**. As shown by the handler's path, take a slightly converging line toward the path to the first tunnel (P3). While your dog is in the tunnel, remain to the left of the center line of the box so that you can take a smoothly converging line toward the path to the second tunnel (P7) while your dog performs the second three-jump sequence.

Do not try to race your dog to the end of the box! If you get to the end of your handling area before your dog does, you will be forced to stop at the boundary. This is likely to cause your dog to hesitate or arc back to you.

Be sure to also work the mirror images of Figures 16-2 through 16-4 off your right.

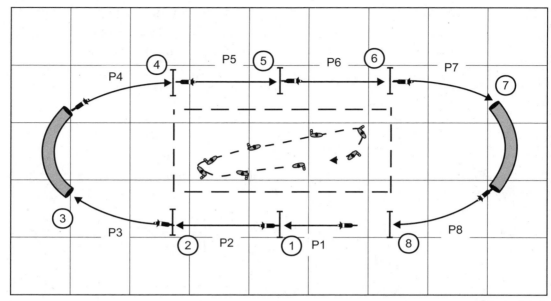

Figure 16-4

IMPORTANT NOTE: *Keep in mind that good distance handling is not loose, lazy, or uninspired. To be a successful distance handler, you must actively work with enthusiasm, precision, and a sense of urgency; smooth, purposeful, and continuous body movements; timely, pro-active commands; and clear, consistent signals. This is one of the most difficult concepts to grasp for people who are used to running alongside their dogs and "powering" them with their legs. Through these and all of the other exercises in this book, you are training your dog to run as fast as he can regardless of how fast you are moving.*

If You Have Problems

Your dog may have **failed to continue ahead or pulled off an obstacle**. This can happen if you stop abruptly at the edge of the handling area. Plan your handling path so that you will not be trapped at the edge of the box with nowhere to go. If you do reach the boundary, come to a gradual stop with one foot ahead of the other, your signaling arm fully extended, and with all body parts facing the path you want your dog to take. Many people tend to stop at the handling line with both feet firmly planted together. Even worse, some plant one foot at the line and then take a lateral side-step with the other. Both actions can cause your dog to come in toward you rather than continue ahead.

Pulling off an obstacle can also happen if you **face the next obstacle rather than the path**. If your dog bypasses an obstacle, freeze and look down at your feet to see where your body was facing.

A common way to get into trouble is to race ahead and meet your dog near the end of the first tunnel as shown in **Figure 16-5**. Racing ahead makes it difficult to get into position to face the path for the second tunnel (P7). As a result, your dog is likely to arc back toward you rather than continue ahead.

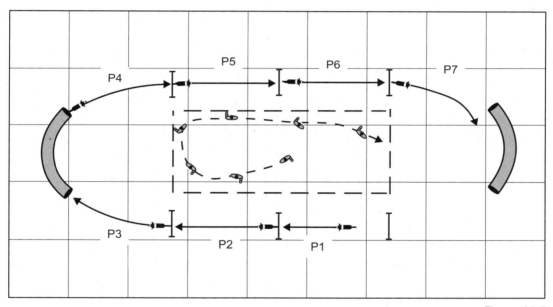

Figure 16-5

You may also have caused the problem through **late commands**. When working at a distance, your verbal commands become even more important than when you are working closer to your dog. If your dog head-checks you between obstacles, it is a good indication that your commands are late. Step up the pace, and if possible, work with a friend to improve your command timing.

If, despite well-timed commands and smooth and accurate body cues, you still have problems, take steps to ensure success on the next try by doing one or more of the following:

♦ Handle somewhat closer, and then gradually increase your distance after each successful attempt.

♦ Use a target at the end of the sequence and try backchaining, adding one obstacle at a time until your dog can perform the entire sequence.

♦ Move the obstacles closer together to make it easier for your dog to succeed. Then, gradually move them apart to their original positions.

Control Work Through Variations

Now that you have patterned your dog to run the entire racetrack in both directions, it is time to introduce some variations to work on control.

Start with the sequence shown in **Figure 16-6**. In this exercise, your dog will perform the entire racetrack with the exception of the center jumps on both sides. Begin by facing and signaling toward the path (P1) as you have done in each previous exercise. When your dog is committed to the first jump, give your command to *Come* or whatever command you use to bring your dog in close toward your side. At the same time, bring your left arm straight down toward your side and turn immediately parallel to the path you want your dog to take (toward P2). Remember to keep moving, taking small steps. When your dog has successfully bypassed the second jump, give your *Out* command. At the same time, turn your body and extend your signaling arm (the one closest to your dog) to face the path to the third jump (P3). When your dog sees the third jump, give your *Jump* command, followed by your command and signal for the tunnel. Repeat these steps down the second line of jumps.

Once successful, continue with the variations shown in **Figures 16-7 and 16-8**. Remember to also work all of the exercises in the opposite direction with the dog on your right side.

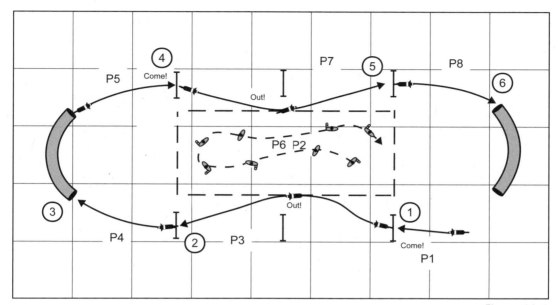

Figure 16-6

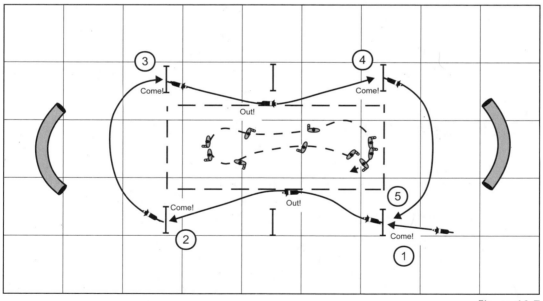

Figure 16-7

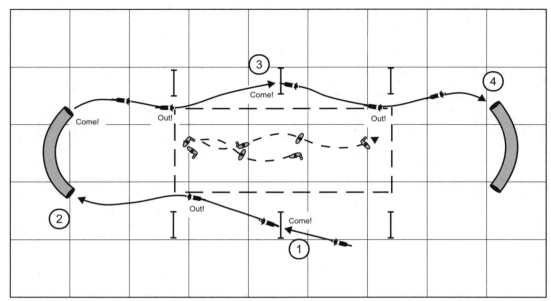

Figure 16-8

Increasing Your Distance

Next, make your handling box smaller so that your dog must work at a greater distance from you as shown in **Figure 16-9**. As the box becomes smaller, it is even more critical that you continue to face the path between obstacles and that you continue to take small walking steps.

Racetracks From the End

Once you are successful handling the racetrack from a center position, increase the challenge by handling from one end. First establish a handling box that ends midway between the first and second jump as shown in **Figure 16-10**. Pattern the sequence in both directions. When handling from the end, it is especially crucial to take a converging path down both lines of jumps. It is also critical that your commands are on time.

When you are successful, decrease the size of the box so that you are limited to remaining behind the first jump as seen in **Figure 16-11**.

Next, introduce variations to keep your dog alert and attentive to your cues as shown in **Figures 16-12 through 16-15**. Use your imagination to devise other variations.

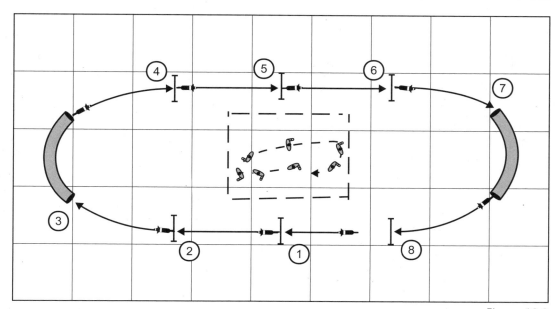

Figure 16-9

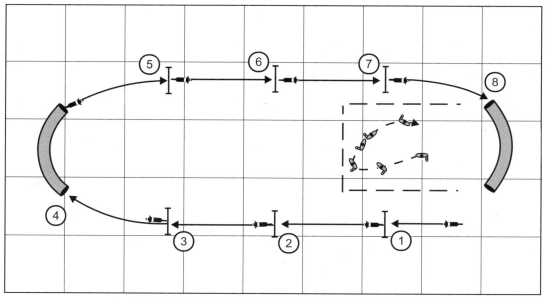

Figure 16-10

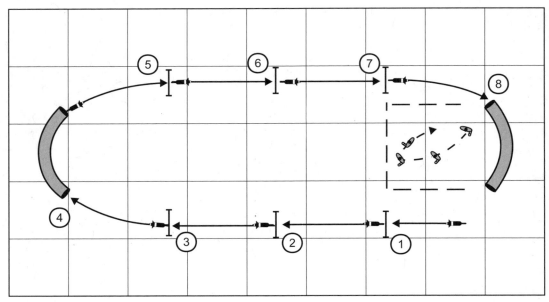

Figure 16-11

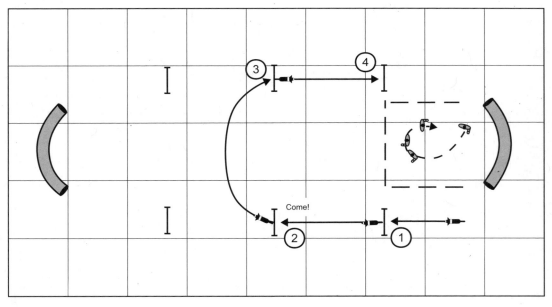

Figure 16-12

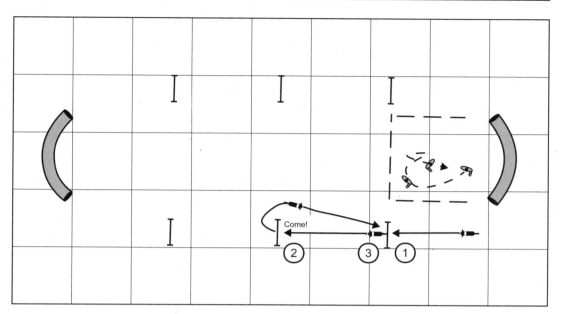

Figure 16-13

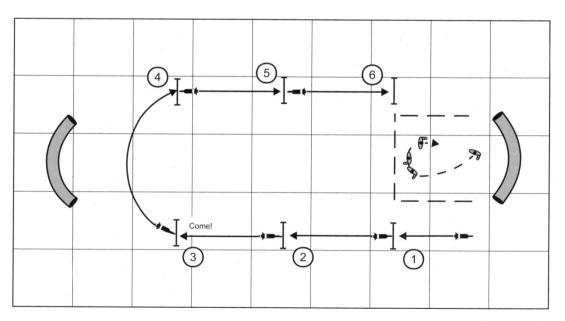

Figure 16-14

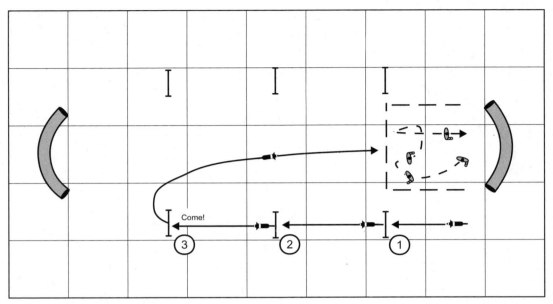

Figure 16-15

Chapter Seventeen

Pinwheels at a Distance

A common element in many agility courses is a jump configuration called a pinwheel. A pinwheel consists of three or more jumps arranged in a circle. An example of a three-jump pinwheel is shown in **Figure 17-1**.

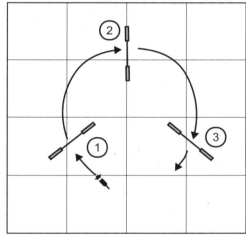

The ability to send your dog to complete a pinwheel while you remain outside of it affords you several competitive advantages. It allows you to get ahead of your dog to better indicate the upcoming sequence of obstacles. It also gives you the freedom to switch sides ahead of your dog while he is performing the pinwheel.

Figure 17-1

How to Begin

To master this valuable (and fun!) maneuver, we will use the setup shown in **Figure 17-2**. Start by working through the three-jump pinwheel while you remain outside of a line made by jumps #1 and #3, as shown in **Figure 17-3**. Command and signal your dog through the first two jumps. Take only small steps, so you will be able to move continuously, always facing the path you want your dog to take. (For example, when your dog is in midair over the first jump, you should be facing midway between the first and second jump, as shown by the path marker P.) When he has committed to jump #2, command *Come* and turn parallel to the path you want him to take. Give your command for the third jump the moment your dog sees it.

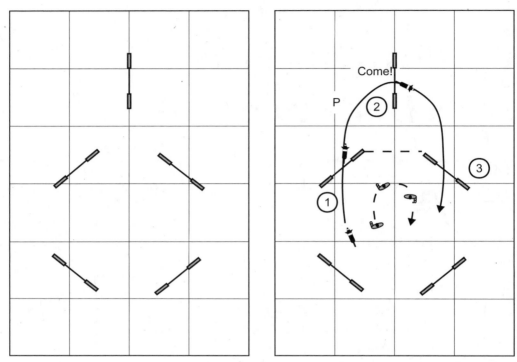

Figure 17-2   Figure 17-3

TRAINING TIP: *With pinwheels, as well as all other sequences, you will communicate best with your dog if you keep moving—rather than starting and stopping—whenever possible. When you keep your body moving in a smooth and controlled path, you are constantly giving your dog information about where you want him to go. When you stop moving, you cease giving him any directional information with your body cues. This can cause your dog to check back with you for reassurance, or to make an incorrect decision about the path you want him to take.*

If You Have Problems

Your dog may have been **reluctant to move out ahead of you**. If this happens, try patterning the sequence by running into the pinwheel with your dog as close as necessary. Then, gradually take a wider handling path on successive tries. Using a toy-on-a-stick (illustrated in **Chapter 15: Combining Flips and Layering**) in your signaling hand can also be helpful for getting your dog to work ahead of you. It can also help you pattern yourself to move in a smooth and flowing path.

Alternatively, you could show your dog a target placed after the second jump of the pinwheel (or have a friend deliver a hand-held treat), and then send him ahead of you over the first two jumps. When your dog is patterned and confident, you can eliminate the extra help and complete the three-jump sequence.

Your dog may have **pulled off the second jump**. This can happen if you turn your body too soon (before he has committed to the second jump). If this happens to you, freeze and look down at your feet to see if this was the problem. To direct your dog from jump #1 to jump #2, you should be facing between the two jumps. If your feet are already facing toward jump #2, you have turned too quickly.

When your dog can confidently perform the three-jump sequence ahead of you off your left, as well as the reverse sequence off your right, you are ready to continue ahead to the next step in your training.

How to Progress

Send your dog though the same sequence; except this time, execute a front cross as your dog travels from jump #2 to #3, as shown in **Figure 17-4**. Make sure you keep moving and that you keep your body facing your dog's path. To execute this maneuver smoothly, you must continuously face your dog's path while moving as quickly as possible to the far right side of the wing of jump #3. If you don't reach that destination before your dog takes off for

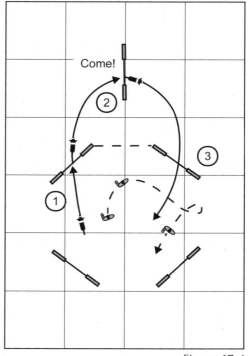

Figure 17-4

the jump, he could easily collide with you or knock the bar of the jump. When this sequence is mastered, perform the mirror image sequence off your right.

Next, add a jump to the beginning and the end of the sequence as shown in **Figure 17-5**. Execute the sequence off your left, as well as the mirror image sequence off your right.

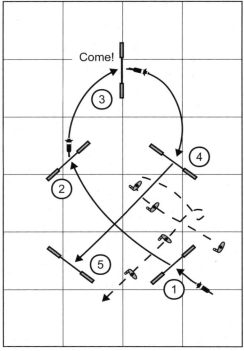

Figure 17-5

If You Have Problems

Your dog may have **pulled off jump #3**. This can happen if you pulled away too soon or too abruptly, or withdrew your signal in an effort to cross in front of jump #4. Try again, this time making an effort to keep your movements smooth and continuous.

Your dog might have **had a run-out to the right of jump #4.** This can happen if you wait too long to move to your right; from your dog's point of view, you are telling him to run around the jump.

Adding a Rear Cross

To make the exercise more challenging, you can begin your approach to the sequence with a rear cross, as shown in **Figure 17-6**.

If You Have Problems

You may have **gotten a spin in the wrong direction** after jump #2. This can happen if you run up too close to the jump as you cross behind. This can also happen if you remain far enough back but fail to move to your right as your dog commits to jump #2. To cue your dog to turn right, you need to be to the right of the center of the jump by the time he commits to the jump.

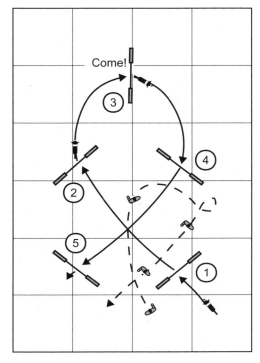

Additional Challenges

Figure 17-6

When you have mastered this exercise, gradually increase the distance to the far jump of the pinwheel. Work until your dog is comfortable running out by himself to a jump that is 30' away. When he can do this with confidence in your training sessions, you can be reasonably sure that he will be successful at a trial, where the jumps are typically 18' to 24' away.

Next, add two additional jumps to your exercise setup as shown in **Figure 17-7**. Now try handling the pinwheel from behind jumps #2 and #6. Start even with your dog, so it will be easy for you to hang back. If you have a very fast dog, this may very well be your most efficient handling strategy if you are even with or behind your dog to start. Just as important, you can't help but have fun when you can handle smoothly from this distance!

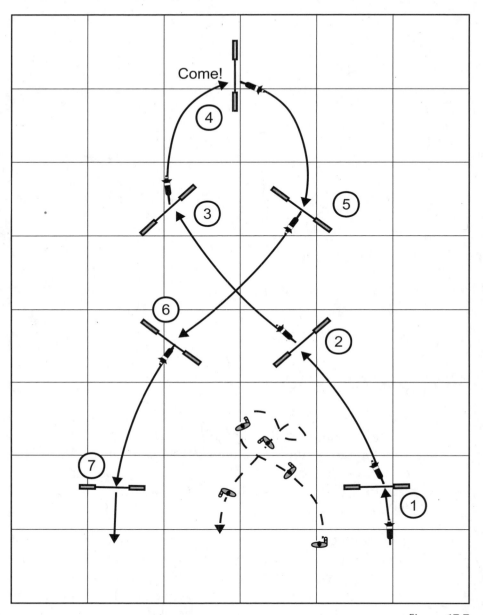

Figure 17-7

Chapter Eighteen

Getting the Opposite End of the Tunnel at a Distance

A very common course challenge is one in which the dog takes a jump or other obstacle and is in a direct line with an incorrect tunnel entrance. The handler is challenged to quickly direct his dog to the opposite end of the tunnel without wasting time, incurring an off-course fault, or getting a refusal. The more speed the dog has as he heads for the incorrect tunnel entrance, the more challenging it is for the handler to redirect him.

Using the exercise setup shown in **Figure 18-1**, you can provide increasingly fast approaches while learning to handle this maneuver from a distance. If you have a speedy dog and you are a slow- to average-speed runner, you will definitely need to master this skill at a distance. To illustrate this need, imagine you are starting even with your dog (as you might be in the middle of a course) as shown in **Figure 18-2**. If you run forward at full speed in an effort to get past jump #3 to direct your dog to the tunnel, your forward motion will cue your dog to take the incorrect tunnel entrance before you ever arrive.

A more successful solution would be to hang back and use a "steering" turn, (concurrent with a *Come* command) turning your body parallel to the path you want your dog to take as seen in **Figure 18-3**. A great advantage of using a steering-based handling strategy is that the same cue works wherever you happen to be in relation to your dog. What's more, you do not need to know ahead of time precisely where you will be when your dog begins his turn. You need only give your command and turn your body, from wherever you are, when you want your dog to turn.

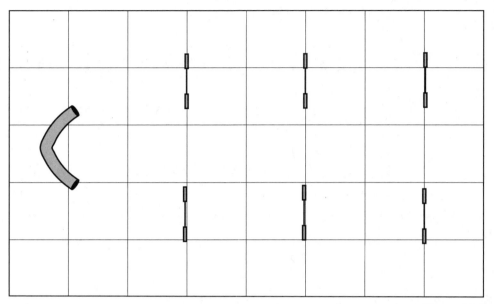

Figure 18-1

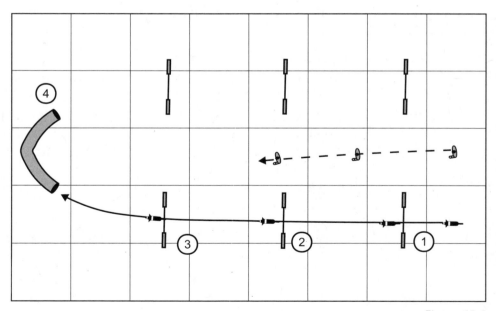

Figure 18-2

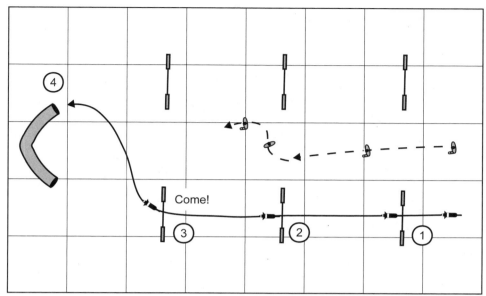

Figure 18-3

How to Begin

Position your dog at an angle to the jump, as shown in **Figure 18-4,** to help ensure early success. Try to confine your handling to within the dashed handler lines. You will be using tight, controlled movements of your body rather than long strides and running feet to direct your dog.

Give your command and signal for the jump. As your dog takes off, give your *Come* command and turn your entire body parallel to the path you want your dog to take (facing path marker P1). At the same time, bring your signaling arm down to your side and close to your body. The moment your dog has turned, give your *Tunnel* command as you smoothly extend your signaling arm ahead of you and straighten out your body toward path marker P2.

Next try the same sequence again, however, this time try to handle from behind the first jump as seen in **Figure 18-5**.

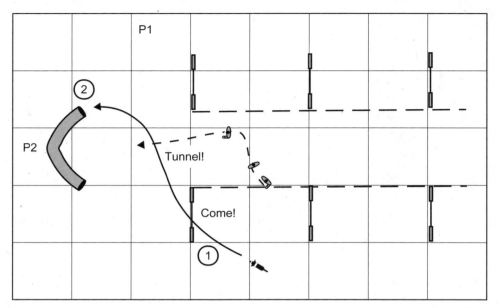

Figure 18-4

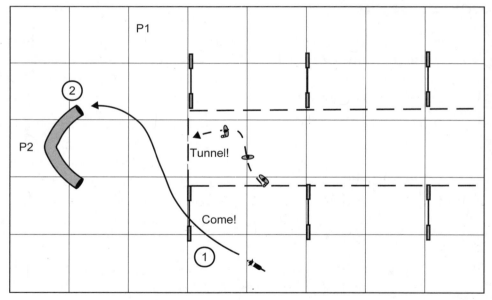

Figure 18-5

If You Have Problems

A very common problem is the dog that **enters the incorrect end of the tunnel** because he never turned to face the correct end. This may have happened because:

- ◆ You were **late with your *Come* command.**

- ◆ Your dog was **not responsive to your well-timed *Come* command.** If this is the case, have someone block the incorrect tunnel entrance and work on rewarding immediate responses to your *Come* command after your dog has performed the jump.

- ◆ You drove your dog into the incorrect end of the tunnel by **moving forward instead of turning your shoulders** and hanging back as your dog approached the jump.

- ◆ You tried to **use your running feet instead of your shoulders** and short steps and ended up facing the path to the incorrect end of the tunnel. This is a common problem. The handler runs to the end of the tunnel he wants and looks back at his dog. At this moment the handler is facing toward the path for the end of the tunnel he does not want as seen in **Figure 18-6**. Resist the urge to beat your dog to the tunnel and use your shoulders to turn your dog in the desired direction.

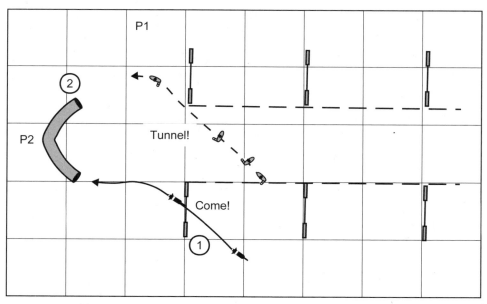

Figure 18-6

Another common problem is that your dog may have made the turn successfully but **bypassed the correct end of the tunnel.** This most often occurs if the handler does not straighten out to face path marker P2 immediately after the dog turns, as shown in **Figure 18-7**. Remember not to focus on or drive toward the tunnel opening you want your dog to take. Instead, face the path and your dog will make a tight turn and know where to go.

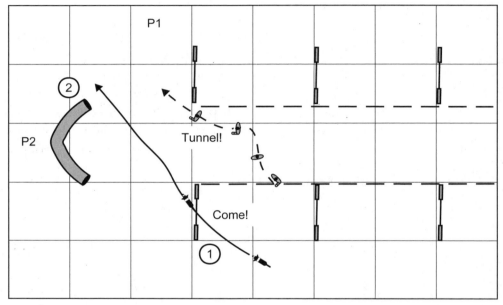

Figure 18-7

How to Progress

If successful, repeat the *Jump-Come-Tunnel* sequence. This time start your dog in a line square with the first jump, as shown in **Figure 18-8**. This variation makes it more challenging for your dog to turn to the correct tunnel opening. Work the mirror image of this and all future exercise variations off the right before progressing to the next step.

Add speed preceding the turn by starting your dog two jumps before the turn to the tunnel. Help your dog succeed by handling from the same starting position as your previous attempt as illustrated in **Figure 18-9**.

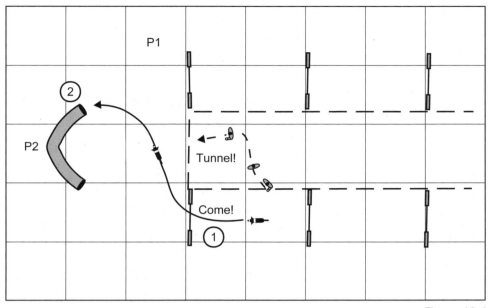

Figure 18-8

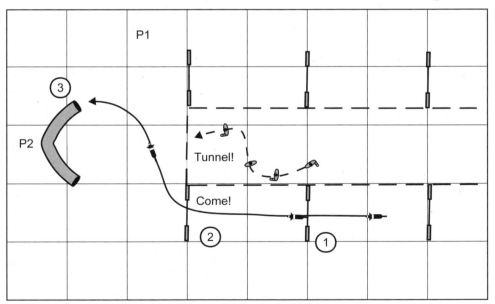

Figure 18-9

If successful, add even more speed by performing three jumps before the turn as shown in **Figure 18-10**. To help your dog succeed, however, remain handling from your previous position.

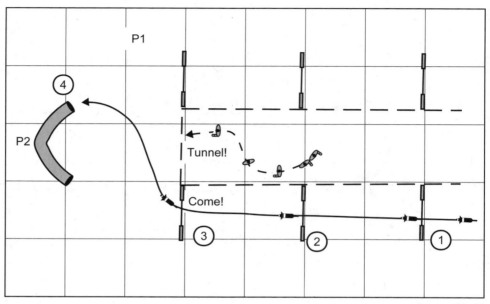

Figure 18-10

Next, reduce your lead-out so that you are starting between jumps #1 and #2 as shown in **Figure 18-11**. This will require you to handle the turn to the correct tunnel opening at high speed and from a greater distance.

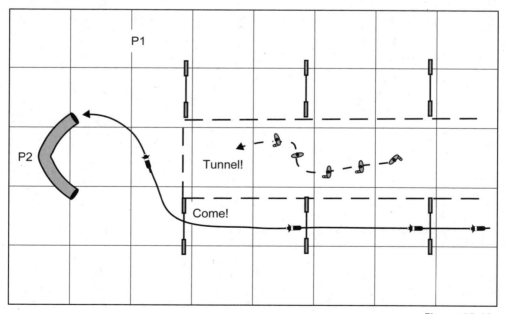

Figure 18-11

Finally, begin without a lead-out, as if you were starting within the body of a course and could not get ahead of your dog, as illustrated in **Figure 18-12**. Make sure you turn your body when your dog needs to turn, regardless of how close or far you are from your dog, as he executes the turn to the correct tunnel opening.

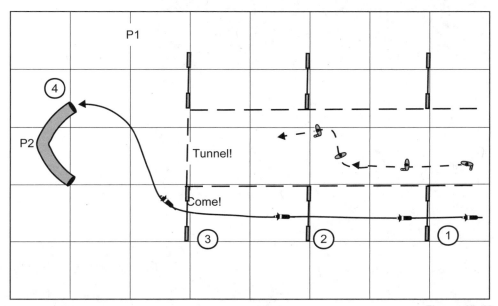

Figure 18-12

Remember to work through the mirror images of each exercise off the right as well as off the left.

RANDALL KNAPP

Chapter Nineteen

Driving Ahead After Tunnels

I'm sure that most of you can relate to this scenario. You arrive at a trial, pick up your course maps, sit down to start obsessing, and suddenly utter words to the effect of "Oh-my-gosh!" (Sometimes the utterances aren't quite so polite.) You wonder if the judge was having a bad day when he designed it; or perhaps he has extremely slow dogs and wouldn't understand your concern; or maybe he just thought it would be sadistically fun to watch handlers of all ages, shapes, and sizes attempt to sprint across the entire length of the ring in 90-degree-plus weather. Not to worry. There is a way to handle nearly every evil challenge with the right skills in your toolbox.

Consider the example shown in **Figure 19-1**. Assume that sequence A through E is within the body of a course and you do not have the advantage of starting ahead of your dog. Using skills such as lateral distance and layering can help you get as far ahead as possible to help your dog find jump E.

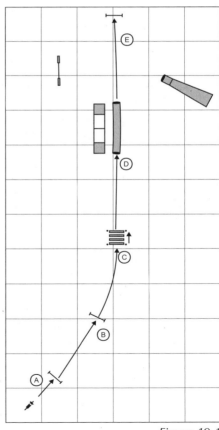

Figure 19-1

Chances are, however, that despite relying on these skills, many handlers will find themselves behind their dogs as they exit the tunnel. To achieve the smoothest run and the fastest time, we want a dog who will drive ahead to jump E at his fastest speed. This means no time-wasting head-checks and no arcing back and incurring a possible refusal or off-course fault. These unwanted possibilities are even more likely when options are present, such as the winged jump and chute shown in Figure 19-1, and when the distance to the correct "straight-ahead" obstacle (jump E) is longer than average.

Tunnels present a greater challenge than other obstacles when it comes to "steering from the rear." In a tunnel, your dog cannot make use of his excellent peripheral vision. (Anyone who has been training agility for any length of time has most certainly observed their dog's keen use of peripheral vision. It often appears as if dogs have eyes in the back of their heads. You suddenly drop your signal while handling from directly behind your dog and he checks back to you for direction.) When in a tunnel—open or closed—your dog is deprived of peripheral vision when determining where to go next. He must rely on your well-timed verbal command and his training to complete the upcoming sequence smoothly, without head-checks, and at his fastest speed.

How to Begin

To teach this skill, start with the setup shown in **Figure 19-2**. Notice the tight 15' spacing between obstacles and the short tunnel—all intended to help your dog be successful from the get-go. Also note that there are no options after completing the tunnel—only the correct obstacle is present.

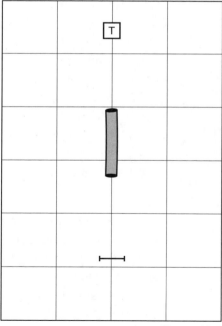

Figure 19-2

Start by backchaining the sequence. Show your dog a treat placed on a target on the back side of the table (or place a favorite toy there). Send him to the table on one command and signal as shown in **Figure 19-3**. As he takes off for the table, release him to the target or toy with a command to *Get It*. Do not ask for a sit or a down. The *Get It* is a release and signals the end of the exercise.

Next, start behind the tunnel as shown in **Figure 19-4**. Just before your dog exits the tunnel, give your command for the table and then a command to *Get It*.

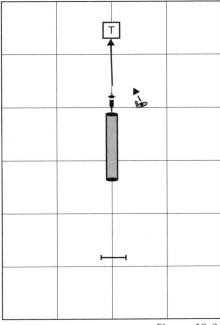

Figure 19-3

Notice that the handler's path converges with the dog's path. When handling a long straight-line sequence and directing your dog from the rear, a converging handling path helps the dog see the line.

If successful, begin behind the jump as shown in **Figure 19-5**.

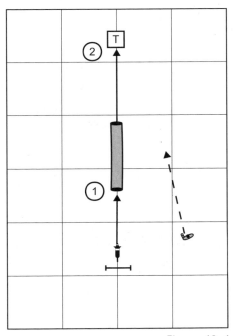

Figure 19-4

If You Have Problems

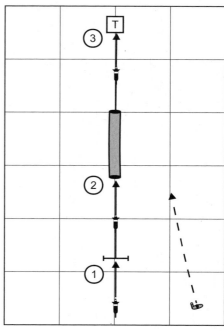

Your dog may have **checked back with you for direction** rather than continuing ahead. Regardless of the reason, break off the exercise with your non-verbal correction such as *Uh-Oh, Oops,* or *Wrong*. Do not repeat your command for the next obstacle. This will only teach your dog to check back with you in the future which will result in wasted time and possible refusals. Check-backs can occur if you:

Figure 19-5

♦ drop your signal abruptly before your dog has committed to the next obstacle. Remember, your dog has excellent peripheral vision. If this is the case, on your next attempt, maintain your signal until your dog is committed to the obstacle.

♦ give a late command for the next obstacle. If this is the problem, work with a friend to improve your command timing.

If, despite excellent handling on your part, your dog fails to continue ahead, you can assume he lacks the confidence to complete the exercise. Make it easier to succeed on the next try by showing him a great reward on the target before beginning, and/or by shortening the distance between obstacles. Jackpot a successful performance with an extra-special reward and additional playtime.

Increase Obstacle Spacing

Once your dog is flawless at performing the exercise shown in Figure 19-5 with 15′ spacing between obstacles, gradually increase the spacing as well as the length of the tunnel until your dog is sailing through the sequence with 22′ spacing and an 18′ tunnel as seen in **Figure 19-6**. Work through the same exercise with the dog on your right side.

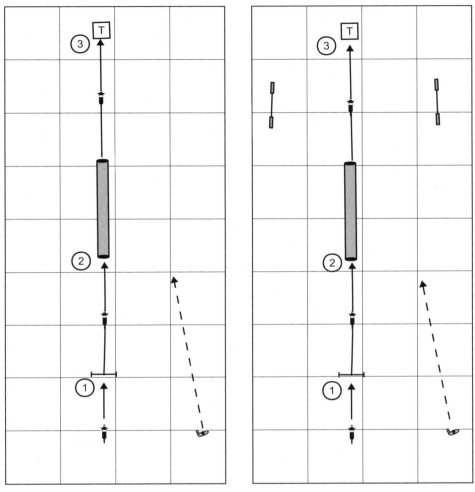

Figure 19-6   *Figure 19-7*

Add Choices

Next, add choices to the right and left of the table as shown in **Figure 19-7**. Repeat the jump-tunnel-table sequence, handling from behind. If your dog makes a mistake (despite good handling) and arcs to one of the side choices, make it easier to succeed by reminding your dog about the target and/or decreasing the distance between obstacles.

As your dog catches on, you should be able to wean away the use of the target. If necessary, you can bring it back later if your dog seems confused or loses confidence.

Work Through Variations

Once your dog is running quickly to the table and ignoring the jumps, it is time to start varying the sequence as shown in **Figures 19-8 and 19-9** (as well as their mirror images off your right). Working through variations will teach your dog to pay attention to your commands rather than operating on his own. Give big rewards for promptly following your directives!

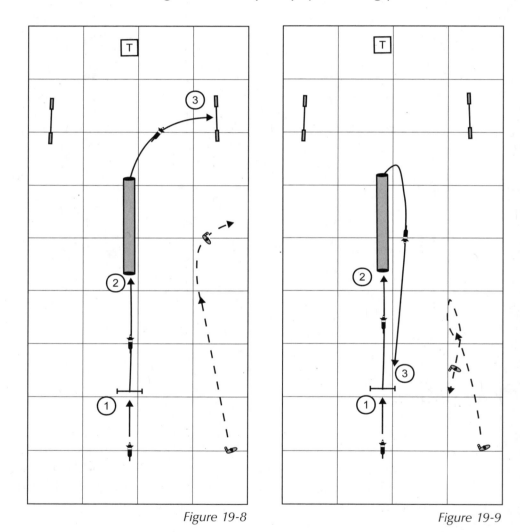

Figure 19-8   Figure 19-9

You've probably guessed what comes next. That's right—the original straight-line sequence in Figure 19-7. If your dog soars smoothly to the table, in spite of the fact that you called him off and rewarded him several times previously, you have accomplished your goal.

Substitute Obstacles

Next, set up similar sequences using different obstacles. For example, substitute a jump for the table as shown in **Figure 19-10,** or substitute a closed tunnel for the open tunnel as in **Figure 19-11**. Use your imagination and have fun!

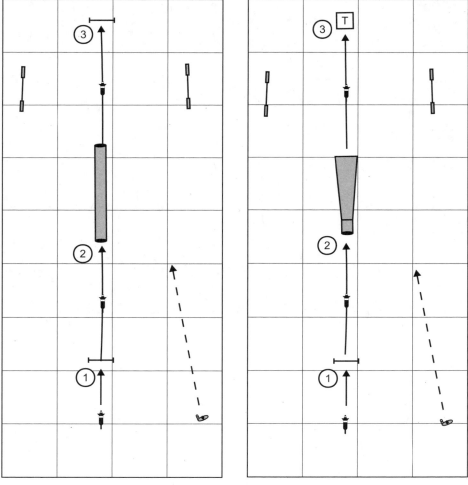

Figure 19-10   Figure 19-11

RANDALL KNAPP

Chapter Twenty

Putting It All Together

N ow that you have mastered a wide variety of foundation skills for your distance training, it is time to put those skills together in more complex sequences handled at a distance. In this chapter you will work through four exercise setups. Each setup provides opportunities to handle sequence variations from behind a specified handler line. Such challenges are sometimes called *Gambles*, *Jokers*, or *Send Bonuses*, and are part of many agility titling programs. Therefore, if you plan to participate in these classes, you and your dog will need to master gambles at a variety of levels. Even more important, working through gamble exercises is extremely valuable for developing distance skills that can give you a competitive advantage in any type of agility course—in any venue.

For all of the exercises that follow, keep the following in mind:

♦ If your dog takes an incorrect obstacle, abort the attempt with a happy attitude and try again. On the next attempt, make sure that your commands and body cues are well-timed and unambiguous. If your dog continues to choose an incorrect obstacle, despite good handling on your part, temporarily block the wrong choice on the next attempt and reward the sequence you are looking for. Then, gradually remove the extra help.

♦ Avoid getting caught at the line with nowhere to go. You will be much more successful at communicating with your dog if you continue to move smoothly and freely, without stopping abruptly. When you stop moving, you stop giving very helpful information to your dog.

- ◆ Be proactive with your body movements. Don't stop or slow down and wait for your dog to turn—keep moving smoothly and deliberately and expect your dog to follow your cue.

- ◆ Imagine that you are holding a pen or a paintbrush in your signaling hand. Then visualize drawing the line you want your dog to take on the ground with one smooth stroke. Since you will be signaling with the hand closest to your dog, you will need to transfer your pen from one hand to the other. When doing this, work to maintain a smooth and continuous line. Further imagine a pen that will deposit a pool of ink if left too long in any one place. You are striving for an even-thickness line without any breaks or jaggedness.

- ◆ In your training sessions, if you find yourself too close to the line, simply ignore it and continue moving smoothly to help your dog be successful. On the next try, make a point of planning your handling path to remain entirely behind the line.

- ◆ If your dog does not continue smoothly to the next obstacle—for example, he stops and checks back with you or spins—do not give extra commands. Instead, break off the exercise and make it easier on the next try by placing the obstacles closer together, by using targets or barriers, or by handling closer to your dog.

Gamble Setup #1

The exercise setup is shown in **Figure 20-1.**

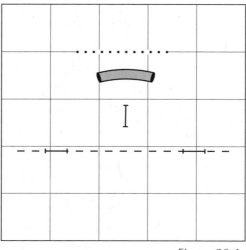

Figure 20-1

Start with the simple sequence of jumps shown in **Figure 20-2**. When your dog leaves the ground for jump #1 he is in a direct line with the off-course tunnel, so be sure to give your *Come* command when he commits to the jump. At the same time, lead with your shoulder and turn parallel to the path you want your dog to take. As he commits to jump #2, again turn parallel to the desired path and give your *Come* command, followed by the command for the #3 jump as soon as he sees it. If successful, perform the mirror image of this sequence off your right.

Layering the Center Jump

Now that you have patterned the jump sequence in both directions, layer the center jump as shown in **Figure 20-3.** The body cues and verbal commands you will use are quite different from the ones you used previously for the three-jump sequence.

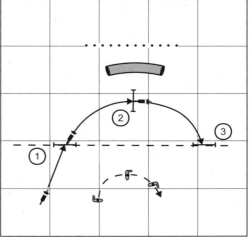

Figure 20-2

When your dog commits to jump #1, give your command for the tunnel while signaling with a fully extended arm toward the path (indicated by path marker P). As your dog exits the tunnel, command *Come* while turning to face parallel to the desired path as shown. Give your command for #3 the moment he sees it. Once you are successful, work the exercise in the opposite direction off your right.

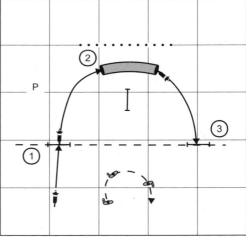

Figure 20-3

Figure-Eights

Next, mix it up with some figure-eights, incorporating an outward flip to the tunnel **(Figure 20-4).** Begin as you did for the sequence in Figure 20-2; however, when your dog commits to jump #2 give your *Out* command and use your left signaling arm to smoothly flip your dog into the tunnel. As he exits, give your *Come* command, do a front cross, and finish with jumps #4 and #5 off your left. Work the exercise in both directions.

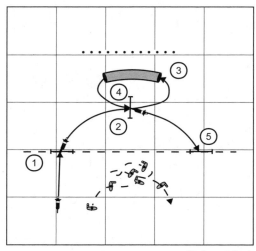

Figure 20-4

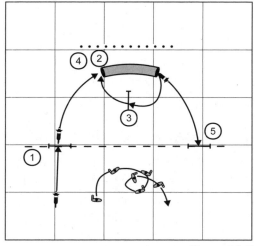

Figure 20-5

Spirals

Next, try a spiral as shown in **Figure 20-5.** Begin as you did for the sequence in Figure 20-3; however, as your dog exits the tunnel, command *Come* and mold the turn back to #3; then perform an outward flip to the #4 tunnel and finish with jump #5. Do the reverse sequence off the right.

Adding the Weave Poles

By now you've noticed the set of twelve weave poles lurking behind the tunnel. Having mastered some of the easier layering sequences, it's time to incorporate the weave poles. To start, move the handling line to the edge of the tunnel and perform the sequence shown in **Figure 20-6.** Be sure to face path marker P—not the weave poles—as you command and signal your dog to weave. As your

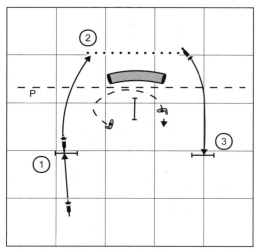

Figure 20-6

dog exits the poles, command *Come* and then command and signal jump #3.

If your dog has trouble with the weave-pole entry, despite proper handling on your part, use wire guides to ensure that he enters correctly. Eventually you can eliminate the extra help.

Once successful, move your handler line back to the edge of the center jump **(Figure 20-7)**, then eventually to the edge of jumps #1 and #3 **(Figure 20-8).**

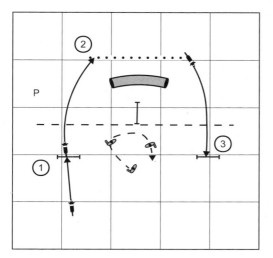

Figure 20-7   Figure 20-8

Next, work on an outward flip from the tunnel to the weave poles. Begin with the handling line positioned at the edge of the tunnel, as shown in **Figure 20-9.** When planning your handling path, remember to give yourself plenty of room to make a smooth U-turn back to the weave poles without becoming trapped by the handling line.

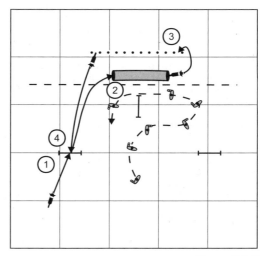

Figure 20-9

Once you're successful, move the handling line to the edge of the second jump as in **Figure 20-10.** Finally, move the handling line to a position in line with jump #1 **(Figure 20-11).** Perform the mirror image of these exercises off your right.

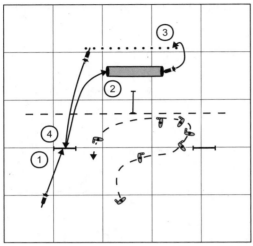
Figure 20-10

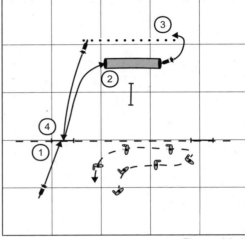
Figure 20-11

Gamble Setup #2

The exercise setup is shown in Figure **20-12.** Note the three dashed handler lines labeled A, B, and C. Your goal is to be able to handle all of the exercise variations from behind Line C. For each exercise you will build confidence and help ensure early success by first handling from behind Line A. When this is mastered, you will progress to handling from behind Line B, and then ultimately from behind Line C.

After each exercise variation, work through the mirror image of the sequence, handling off your right.

Racetracks

Start with the "racetrack" sequence shown in **Figure 20-13.** When handling from behind Line A, you will be layering the weave poles as your dog completes jumps #4 and #5. To help ensure success, be sure to face path marker P1 when your dog commits to jump #2. As he exits the tunnel, face path marker P2. Concentrate on giving well-timed, enthu-

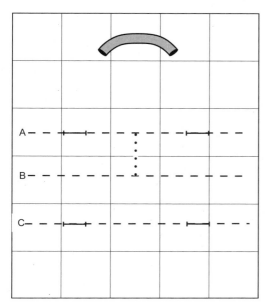

Figure 20-12

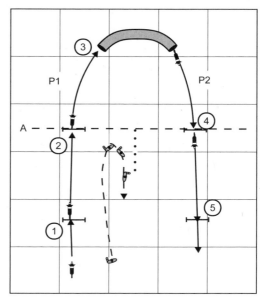

Figure 20-13

siastic commands. Watch for head-checks. They usually indicate your commands are late. If this exercise is still difficult for you, review the exercises in ***Chapter 16: Distance Racetracks.***

Once you are successful, handle from behind Line B as shown in **Figure 20-14.**

Finally, remain behind Line C as your dog completes the sequence **(Figure 20-15).**

Opposite Ends of the Tunnel

Handling from behind Line A, work through the sequence shown in **Figure 20-16.** As your dog approaches jump #2, hang back (with signal arm still extended) to cue the upcoming turn. As he takes off, give your

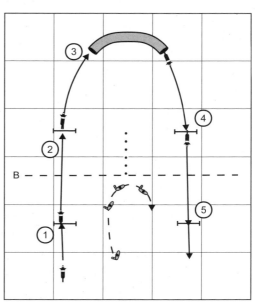

Figure 20-14

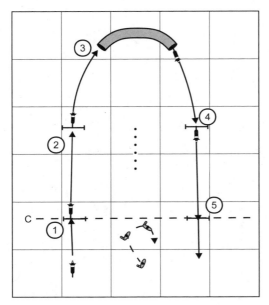

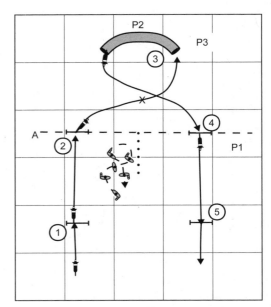

Figure 20-15   *Figure 20-16*

Come command and turn your entire body parallel to the path you want your dog to take (facing path marker P1). At the same time, bring your signaling arm down to your side and close to your body. When your dog has turned and has reached position X (the point at which the dog's path needs to turn), give your *Tunnel* command as you smoothly extend your signaling arm and straighten out your body toward path marker P2.

When your dog enters the tunnel, quickly take a few steps backward so that you will not be stuck at the edge of the handler line when your dog exits. Your ability to move freely will help your dog complete the sequence smoothly and accurately. As he exits, give your *Out* command and signal and step forward toward path marker P3. Give your command for jump #4 the moment he sees it.

Progress to handling the sequence from behind Line B as shown in **Figure 20-17.** You may actually find this easier in some ways, since your movements are not restricted by the position of the weave poles. Note that the position of P1 has changed. At the moment your dog needs to turn, you should face parallel to the path you want him to take. As such, the location of P1 is much different when you handle from farther away.

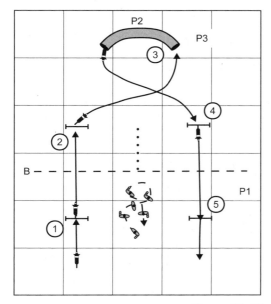

Figure 20-17

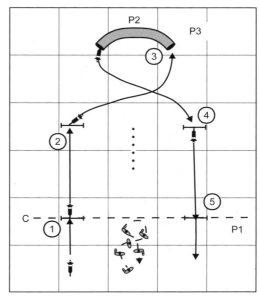

Figure 20-18

Next, handle from behind Line C as shown in **Figure 20-18.** Note the new position of path marker P1.

Bypassing the Tunnel

The next exercise involves by-passing the tunnel and performing a 180-degree turn between jumps #2 and #3 as illustrated in **Figure 20-19.** In this sequence, handling behind Line A is actually more difficult than handling from farther away. Therefore, start by working from behind Line B rather than Line A.

As your dog approaches jump #2, begin to hang back while keeping your signaling arm fully extended. As he takes off, give your *Come* command and move

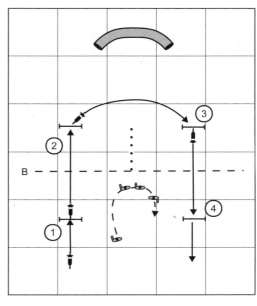

Figure 20-19

laterally to the right. As you do, smoothly trace the line you want your dog to take with your signaling hand (the hand closest to your dog). At the moment he sees jump #3, give your *Jump* command.

If your dog mistakenly takes the tunnel or the weave poles, work with a friend to fine-tune your handling. You can also use barriers to temporarily block the entrances to these obstacles until your dog catches on. Progress to handling from behind Line C using the same handling maneuvers **(Figure 20-20).**

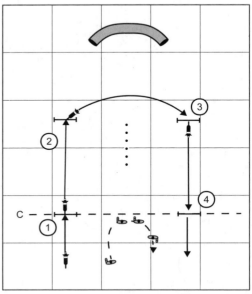

Figure 20-20

Adding the Weave Poles

Next, it's time to add the weave poles. Start with one of the simpler exercises as shown in **Figure 20-21.** Handling from behind Line A, hang back, give your *Come* command and cue a tight turn as your dog approaches jump #2. Give your command to *Weave* the moment your dog sees the poles. As he exits the poles, it is an easy push to jump #4.

If your dog has trouble with the weave-pole entrance or exit, despite good handling on your part, use wire guides at the first and/or last poles to help him be successful. Alternatively, you could replace the six regulation poles with training poles such as offset poles. You can eventually remove the guides or return to

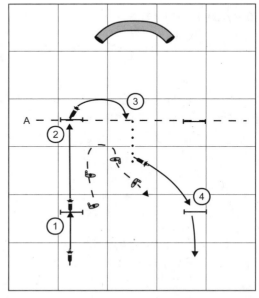

Figure 20-21

using regulation poles. Add distance by repeating the exercise and handling from behind Line B **(Figure 20-22).** Once mastered, progress to handling from behind Line C as shown in **Figure 20-23.**

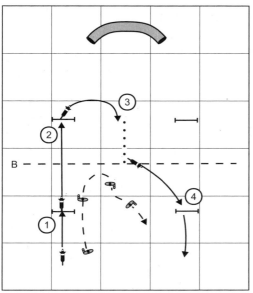

Figure 20-22

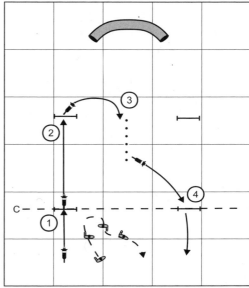

Figure 20-23

Incorporating Outs

Next, try a more challenging sequence **(Figure 20-24).** Begin the same as you did with the previous exercise; however, as your dog exits the weave poles, push him away from you to complete #4 through #7. As your dog exits the poles, use your *Out* command and signal (facing P1) to push to jump #4. As your dog takes off for the jump, face path marker P2 and give your command and signal for the tunnel. Just before your dog exits the tunnel give your command

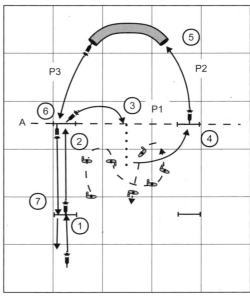

Figure 20-24

and signal for jump #6, facing path marker P3. Add distance by remaining behind Line B **(Figure 20-25),** and then Line C **(Figure 20-26).**

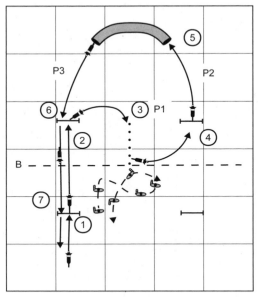

Figure 20-25

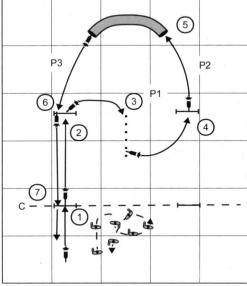

Figure 20-26

Figure Eights

Try a figure-eight pattern as shown in **Figure 20-27.** As your dog takes off for jump #1 give your *Come* command while turning your body parallel to the path you want him to take (facing P1).

When he has turned enough to approach the weave poles, give your command to *Weave* and straighten out your body to face path marker P2. Cross behind the poles and move forward but stay behind your dog as

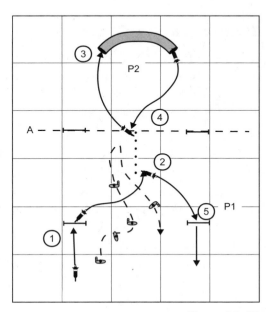

Figure 20-27

he weaves. (If you catch up with him, you will both reach the handling line together, giving you no room to help your dog move ahead to the tunnel.)

As he exits the last pole, give your *Tunnel* command as you continue to move forward. There is no need for a directional command since your dog is facing the correct end of the tunnel as he completes the poles. When he exits, pull your dog to the poles using your *Come* command and give your command to weave as soon as he sees the obstacle. Continue ahead and push him to jump #5.

Next, increase your distance by remaining behind Line B as shown in **Figure 20-28.** As you increase your distance, decrease your lead-out. As you do so, remember that you need to cue the turn from #1 to #2 from wherever you are when your dog needs to turn. It is also helpful to do a front cross while your dog is in the tunnel, as shown. Follow with another front cross between the weave poles and jump #5.

Once you are successful, handle the sequence from behind Line C **(Figure 20-29).** To give yourself maneuvering room, start parallel with your dog and do not lead out.

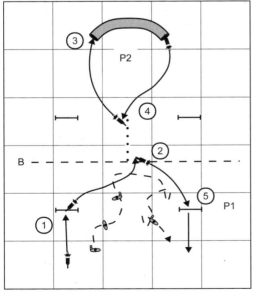

Figure 20-28

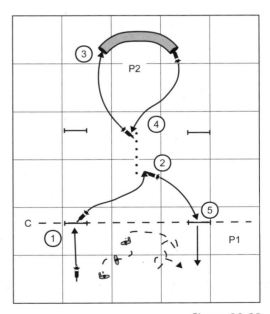

Figure 20-29

An alternate figure-eight pattern is shown in **Figure 20-30.** Begin as before; however, this time handle the weave poles off your left and pull to the #3 tunnel. As your dog exits the tunnel, do a front cross and handle #4 and #5 off your left.

If all goes well, progress to handling from greater distances as shown in **Figures 20-31 and 20-32.**

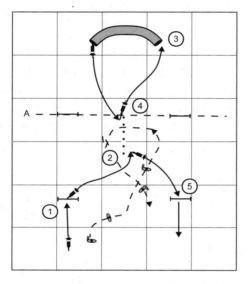

Figure 20-30

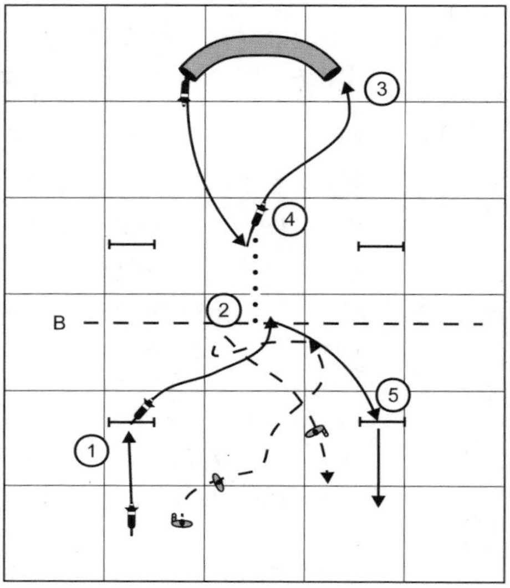

Figure 20-31

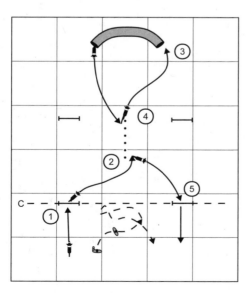

Figure 20-32

Gamble Setup #3

The equipment setup is shown in **Figure 20-33.**

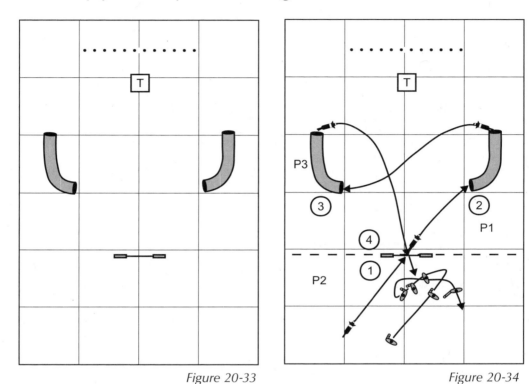

Figure 20-33   *Figure 20-34*

To begin on a successful note, start with the figure-eight-shaped sequence shown in **Figure 20-34.** Position your dog at an angle to #1, so there will be a straight line to #2. Start parallel with your dog but not ahead of him, facing parallel to the path you want him to take (P1).

Handling from behind the handling line, give your command and signal to *Jump.* As your dog commits to the jump, give your *Tunnel* command. Immediately before your dog exits the tunnel, give your *Come* command, bring your signaling arm down to your side, and turn parallel to the path you want him to take (facing P2). When your dog sees the correct tunnel opening, release him to it with your *Tunnel* command while smoothly extending your signaling arm ahead of you (not out to the side) and turning to face P3. As he commits to the tunnel, move laterally to your right.

Immediately before he exits, give your *Come* command and then command and signal #4 off your right.

If this sequence is difficult for you, revisit **Chapter 18: Getting the Opposite End of the Tunnel at a Distance.**

If successful, repeat the mirror image of this sequence (and of all future sequence variations) off your right.

How to Progress

Next, try the sequence shown in **Figure 20-35.** Begin as before, commanding *Come* before your dog exits the tunnel. As he exits, move laterally to your left. At the same time, keep your signaling arm extended, smoothly tracing the line you want him to take. The moment he sees #3, give your *Tunnel* command. As he enters, continue to move to your left. As he exits, command and signal him to #4 off your left as shown.

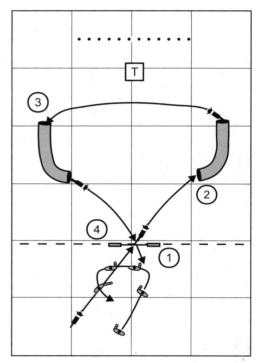

Figure 20-35

Adding the Table

Once you've gotten a flawless performance of the sequence in Figure 20-35, it is time to try another variation as shown in **Figure 20-36.**

Begin as before, however, when your dog enters the tunnel, quickly move to your left. (This will place you in a good position to face path marker P for the table.) Before he exits the tunnel, give your *Come* command, since a turn in your direction is required. When he just begins to turn and can see the table, step forward and push toward P as you give your *Table* command.

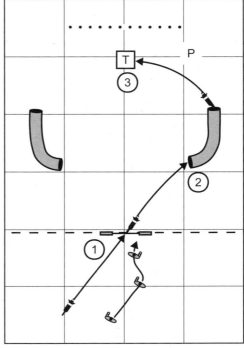

Figure 20-36

NOTE: *When incorporating the table in your distance sequences, it is a good idea to refrain for asking for a sit or down—unless you are 99 percent sure your dog will assume the correct position immediately on your first (and only) command. The reason is, if your dog fails to sit or down immediately, you have lost the opportunity to reward the behavior you are training, which is finding the table at a distance.*

If your dog has trouble finding the table, show him a target on the table before your next attempt, then backchain the sequence. First perform #2 to #3. When successful, perform #1 through #3.

If all goes well, try the variation shown in **Figure 20-37,** which combines elements from Figures 20-34 and 20-36. Start as you did with the sequence in Figure 20-34. When your dog exits the #3 tunnel, push to path marker P and give your command for the table.

Adding the Weave Poles

Now that your dog is sufficiently patterned to turn toward you after exiting the #2 tunnel, it is time to include the weave poles. Try the sequence shown in **Figure 20-38.** Notice that the handling line has been moved closer to the weave poles to help ensure early success and to build confidence.

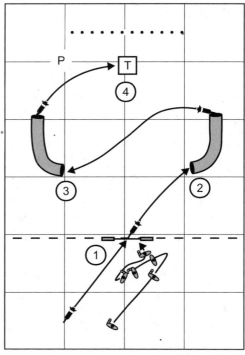

Figure 20-37

You may find it easiest to handle this sequence off your right. Doing so puts you in a great position to face path marker P for the weave poles. Lead out as shown and direct your dog through #1 and #2. Immediately before he exits the tunnel, give your command to *Weave*. (No directional command such as *Come* or *Out* is called for because the weave-pole entrance is directly ahead.) Finish with #4 and #5 off your right.

If your dog has trouble finding the weave poles or the correct entry, examine your handling position and make sure that all parts of your body are facing the path (P). Handlers often signal toward the correct direction, while their feet and torso face another direction entirely.

If your dog still has difficulty despite good handling on your part, help your dog be successful by placing two wire guides at the entrance of the poles to make the correct entry easier to find. Eventually you can eliminate the extra help.

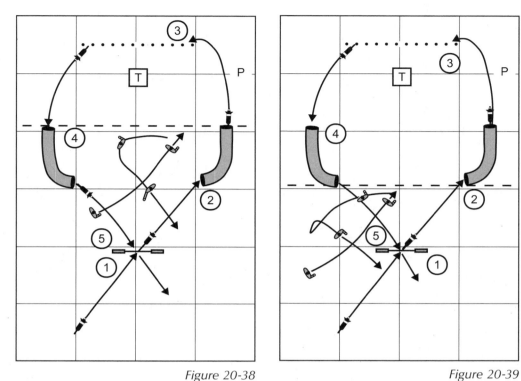

Figure 20-38   *Figure 20-39*

Next, gradually handle the sequence from a greater distance **(Figures 20-39 and 20-40).**

Don't forget to work through the mirror image sequence off the right. This will provide experience sending to a very different weave-pole entry.

How to Progress

At this point, you should be equipped to handle your way through even more variations. Try the sequences in **Figures 20-41 through 20-43.** Or invent your own!

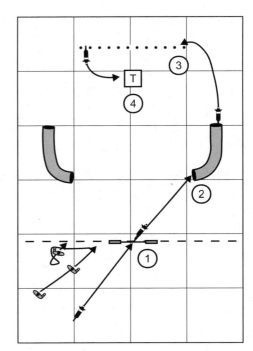

Figure 20-40

Figure 20-41

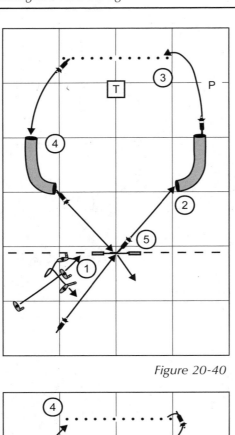

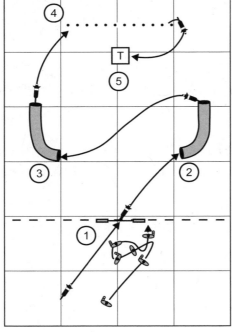

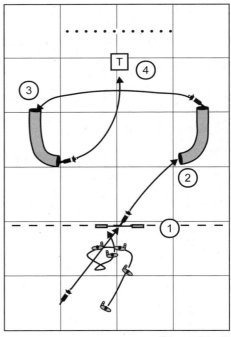

Figure 20-42

Figure 20-43

Gamble Setup #4

The equipment setup is shown in **Figure 20-44.**

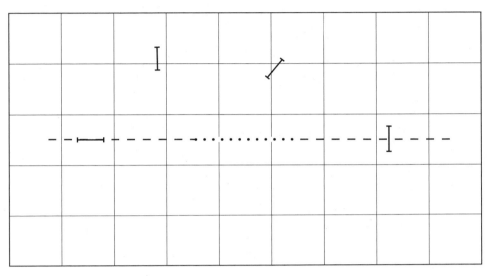

Figure 20-44

How to Begin

Start with the five-obstacle sequence shown in **Figure 40-45.** Help your dog get a tight turn from #1 to #2 by setting him up at an angle to #1 as shown. As your dog commits to #1, give your *Come* command and turn parallel to the path you want him to take. When he has turned, give your command to *Weave* and face between your dog's current position and the entrance to the weave poles (path marker P1).

NOTE: *If you prefer, you could use a false turn or Reverse Flow Pivot (RFP) for the turn to the weave poles instead of the described "steering turn." However, properly executed, a steering turn is often faster and smoother.*

Continue to move ahead but remain at a generous lateral distance as your dog weaves, and resist the urge to get ahead of him. As his nose exits the last pole, give your *Out* command while moving and signaling in a smooth arc toward P2 with your fully extended left arm. As he turns toward #3, smoothly transfer the signal to your right arm and continue to move through the arc. Complete the sequence with #4 and #5 off your right.

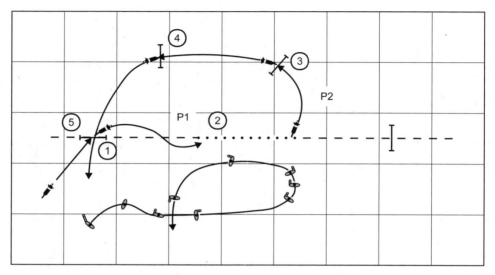

Figure 20-45

If You Have Problems

Your dog may have **made an about-turn after the weave poles** rather than move laterally away from you toward #3. This can happen if you **handle too closely** to the weave poles as shown in **Figure 20-46.** If you are handling closely at the end of the poles, you will not be able to move freely in a wide-arc U-turn. Instead, you must make a tight about-turn, which will encourage your dog to do the same.

This can also happen if you **get too far ahead of your dog** as he weaves **(Figure 20-47).** When your dog reaches the end of the poles you will find it awkward to face the correct path, which can cause a run-out at #3.

If you still have problems despite good handling on your part, make the exercise easier by moving #3 closer to the handling line and/or substituting winged jumps for the wingless jumps. You can also use a target (or a friend enticing your dog with a reward) on the landing side of jump #3. End the exercise after #3. If successful, on future attempts gradually wean away the extra help. Once your dog can perform #1 through #3 without help, you can then resume working through the entire five-obstacle sequence.

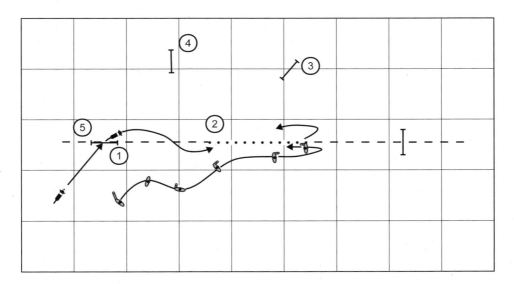

Figure 20-46

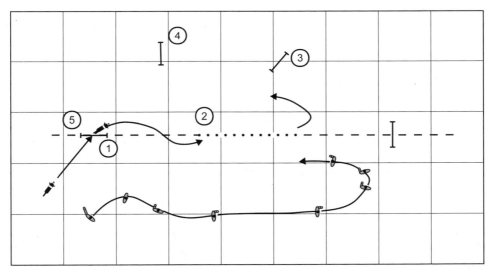

Figure 20-47

Adding a Jump

Next, make the exercise more challenging by adding a jump after the weave poles as shown in **Figure 20-48.** Your goal is to get a tight, outward turn from #3 to #4. Begin as before, handling at a generous lateral distance from the poles, without getting ahead of your dog. As he exits the poles, pull him slightly toward you to set him up for a left turn after #3. Quickly release him to the jump. As he commits to it, give your *Out* command while walking and signaling in a smooth arc toward path marker P with your fully extended left arm. As he turns toward #4, smoothly transfer the signal to your right arm and continue to move through the arc. Complete the sequence with #5 and #6 off your right.

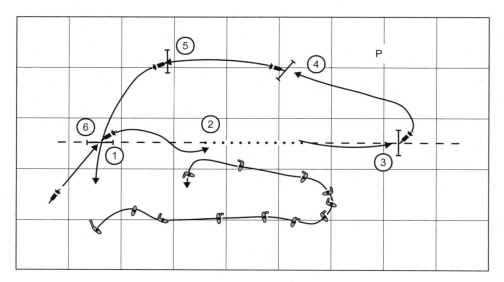

Figure 20-48

If You Have Problems

Your dog may have **had a wide turn to #4** and/or a run-out at #4 **(Figure 20-49)**. The wide turn can be caused by **your running ahead toward #3** as your dog exits the poles. This cues your dog that he will be continuing straight ahead after #3 rather than turning. The run-out can occur because it is awkward to face the correct path from a handling position that is too close to jump #3.

If you still have problems despite proper handling, make the exercise easier by targeting or by moving jumps #4 and #5 closer to the handler line.

Wrapping to the Right

Once you are successful, try the same sequence with a wrap to the right after #3 **(Figure 20-50)**. As your dog exits the poles, bump him outward slightly to set him up for the right turn after #3. Quickly release to the jump. As he commits to it, give your *Come* command and move laterally to your right, tracing the path you want your dog to take with your left signaling arm. As his nose passes to your side of #3, smoothly transfer your signal to your right arm, give your *Out* command and press toward path marker P. When he has turned, give your command for jump #4 and finish the sequence off your right.

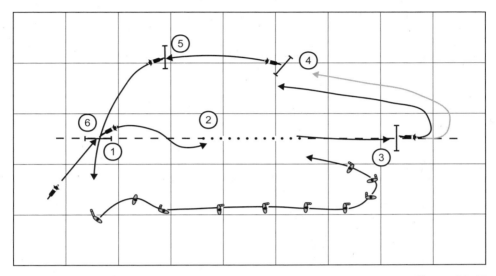

Figure 20-49

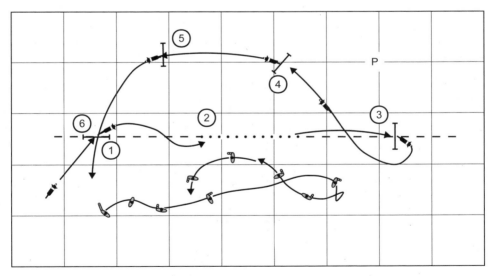

Figure 20-50

If You Have Problems

Your dog may have **failed to find the line to jump #4 (Figure 20-51).** This can easily happen if you **run too close to #3** to execute the wrap. In doing so, you will not be in a good position to face path marker P. Your dog may easily interpret the next obstacle to be the weave poles.

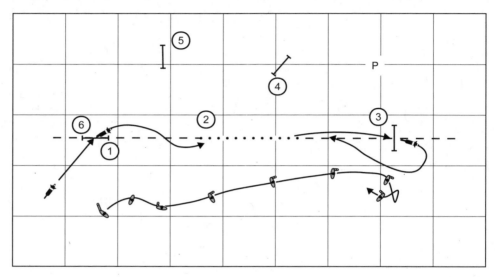

Figure 20-51

Starting Off Your Left

Next, try the sequence shown in **Figure 20-52.** Set up your dog for a straight line between #1 and #2. Start wide from your dog, facing path marker P1. Give your command and signal for #1. As he commits to #1 give your command and signal for #2, facing P2. Continue with #3 off your left, hanging back and shortening your stride to cue the approaching turn. As he commits to #3, give your *Come* command to turn your dog toward #4, while moving laterally to your right and tracing the path you want your dog to take with your left signaling arm. The moment he sees the weave poles, give your command to *Weave*. As he nears the poles, smoothly transfer your signal to your right arm and face the path to the poles shown by path marker P3. Finish with the weave poles off your right.

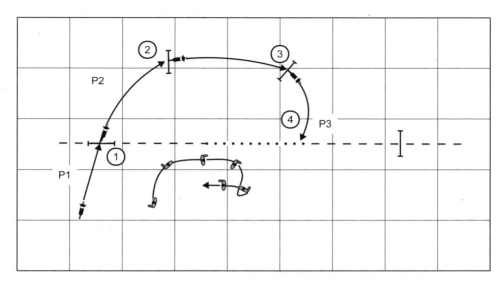

Figure 20-52

If You Have Problems

Your dog may have **had a wide turn** from #3 to #4 **(Figure 20-53)**. This can be caused by **running ahead of #4**, in an attempt to micro-manage the weave-pole entry. As you run ahead (as opposed to slowing down) you are cueing your dog that the next obstacle is likely to be the jump that is ahead of him. This can cause wasted time or a costly off-course fault.

Another common problem is that your dog may have **entered at the second or third pole (Figure 20-54)**. This can happen if you **turn parallel to the weave poles too soon**, rather than facing the path.

Increasing the Difficulty

For all of you overachievers who have mastered each of these exercises as drawn, add to the difficulty by gradually increasing the spacing between obstacles until they are spaced 30' apart. This increases the distance at which you must work from your dog. It also provides you with a challenge that is greater than you will likely encounter in competition. Once you master the exercises under these extreme conditions, you should feel confident to execute these maneuvers in competition when the obstacles are more reasonably spaced.

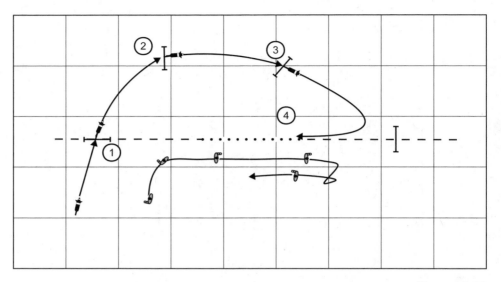

Figure 20-53

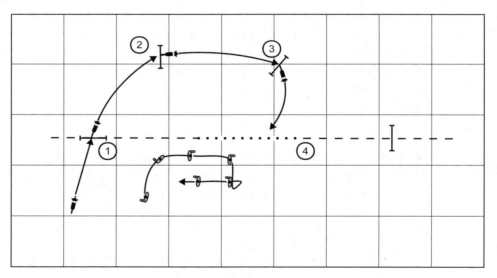

Figure 20-54

Further Resources

The most effective training and handling methods are often a part of a complete "system" of communicating with your dog. The system incorporates a consistent set of cues that are used throughout all of your dog's agility training. Adhering to one comprehensive system, as opposed to mixing elements from vastly different systems, will help your dog learn faster, will help eliminate confusion, and will strengthen your dog's trust in you, his handler. Better trust and understanding results in improved teamwork, smoother runs, and faster times!

If you would like to learn more about Jane Simmons-Moake's training and handling methods (the FlashPaws "system") you may enjoy her other highly acclaimed books and videos:

Excelling at Dog Agility

This three-book series provides a detailed plan from the ground up for training your dog to reach his maximum potential in the sport of agility.

Book 1: Obstacle Training - Updated Second Edition

- ♦ Provides detailed, step-by-step instructions for training your dog to master each agility obstacle with safety, fun, and competitive excellence in mind.

- ♦ Includes important principles for building a happy and successful working relationship with your dog, as well as a solid foundation for all of your agility training.

- ♦ Focuses on setting high standards and getting it right from the start so that no retraining will be necessary later down the road.

Book 2: Sequence Training - Updated Second Edition

- ♦ Teaches you how to sequence smoothly from one obstacle to the next, to reach your dog's highest potential for speed and accuracy.

- ♦ Helps you develop a consistent set of cues for communicating with your dog on the agility course. As a result, your dog will understand your directives in an instant, even at the highest of speeds and the greatest of distances.

- ♦ Provides detailed lesson plans for Beginner, Intermediate I, and Intermediate II agility training classes.

Book 3: Advanced Skills Training - Updated Second Edition

- ♦ Illustrates how to isolate and train many of the higher-level skills necessary to successfully compete at the most advanced levels of competition.

- ♦ Describes how to strengthen and maintain existing skills for attaining fast and reliable performances in the agility ring.

- ♦ Provides in-depth answers to commonly asked questions in a helpful Problem Solving appendix.

Competitive Agility Training with Jane Simmons-Moake

This three-DVD series was namd **Best Video Production of the Year** by the Dog Writer's Association of America. Each DVD is approximately 80 minutes long. Professionally produced by Canine Training Systems, the series features training demonstrations using 26 breeds, 70 dogs, and 43 handlers. Both positive and negative examples are used to illustrate the consequences of handling choices.

DVD 1: Obstacle Training

Learn how to train your dog to master each obstacle with competitive excellence in mind. Includes important principles for building a strong foundation for all of your agility training.

DVD 2: Sequence Training

Discover how to sequence smoothly from one obstacle to the next, to reach your dog's highest potential for speed and accuracy.

DVD 3: Advanced Skills Training

Learn how to isolate and train many of the skills necessary to compete at the highest levels.

Notes: